# UNDER THE ARMOR
## — The Courage to Surrender —

**CANDICE KNIGHT**

# UNDER THE ARMOR
## The Courage to Surrender

**CANDICE KNIGHT**

# UNDER THE ARMOR
## The Courage to Surrender

Copyright © 2025, Candice Knight

*No part of this publication may be reproduced, stored in a retrieval system, or transmitted in any form or by any means—electronic, mechanical, photocopying, recording, or otherwise—except for brief quotations in printed reviews, without prior written permission from the author.*

Cataloguing data available from
**Library and Archives Canada**

First Edition 2025

ISBN | PRINT | 978-1-0693772-0-3
ISBN | DIGITAL | 978-1-0693772-1-0
ISBN | AUDIO | 978-1-0693772-2-7

To learn more about Candice and her work, order additional copies of her book, please visit: candiceknight.ca

# Endorsements

"Candice Knight's Under the Armour is a profound and inspiring work that skillfully blends personal storytelling with practical wisdom. Through her courageous recounting of her own journey through trauma and healing, Candice offers readers not only a mirror to their own struggles but also tools to unlock their authentic selves. The book is both engaging and deeply informative, guiding readers toward self-discovery and emotional openness. It's a must-read for anyone seeking to shed their own armour and live a more connected and genuine life."

— **Tracey Rogers**
*Entrepreneur and Author of*
*Motorcycles, Moose & Magic: The Ride to Self Love*

---

"Under the Armor is the message I didn't know I needed to hear. I've spent the past 40 years of my life trying to be strong, independent and resilient. I wore my armor with pride and I saw it as the hard shell I needed to protect me, but I didn't take the time to get to know the brave little girl underneath. Candice's book walks you through the steps to embracing all of yourself, even the vulnerable parts. True growth and resilience begin with self-acceptance and self-awareness - it's time to love the person you are Under the Armor."

— **Cassandra Aarssen**
*Clutterbug and Host of HGTV's Hot Mess House*

"Candice's insightful life-journey is one of struggles that we all must go through, in some variation or other, to discover who we truly are. Self-discovery and self-worth are vital to our purpose in service to others. In her book, Under the Armor, Candice shares her truly useful wisdom to help us find a guiding light in the often challenging physical world experience."

— **Shawn Leonard**
*Hay House Author of Spirit Talker*

---

"Candice Knight's book, Under the Armor, encourages readers to reflect on their emotional armor, understand its origins, and begin their journey of self-awareness and healing. Through this process, we can cultivate self-compassion, reclaim vulnerability, and live more authentically, freeing ourselves from limiting patterns, and setting a foundation for healthier future generations. This book serves as a guide to navigate our journey, inspiring readers to embrace their inner strength and vulnerability."

— **Dianne Bondy B.Soc.Sc**
*Social Justice Activist & Author*
*Accessible Yoga Teacher*
*Leader of the Yoga For All movement*
*Author, Educator, Disruptor  https://diannebondy.com/*

---

# Dedication

This book is dedicated to —

My children, Marcus, Mya and Lucy,
for choosing me to be your guide,
despite the weight of my armor

My angels,
those in human and spirit form,
for teaching me, challenging me, and staying by me

My dad, George,
who, for better or worse,
made me a Knight in the first place

# Foreword

When I first met Candice, I was fighting battles on all fronts, not just in the ring, but within myself. The world knew me as a boxer, a fighter who could endure physical pain. What they didn't see, though, was the chaos beneath the surface, the storm that raged in my mind and heart. I had wrapped myself in layers of armor, not just to protect my body, but to shield my heart from wounds too deep to confront. I thought life had made me tough, but it wasn't until I started working with Candice that I realized true strength isn't just about endurance — it's about embracing vulnerability, and finding peace in the midst of chaos.

I thought my strength came from my ability to take punches. But it wasn't until I met Candice that I learned real strength comes from confronting your inner battles and facing the vulnerabilities you've buried beneath the armor of survival.

Candice saw past the persona I had built, the physical toughness, and into the wounds I had carried for years. In the beginning, I wanted to run, to retreat behind the armor I had worn for so long. But Candice helped me to face it. She showed me that while my armor protected me, it also kept me from living a full and authentic life.

Candice's question about our armor preventing us from truly living hit me like a blow, one I wasn't prepared for. What if, in my effort to be strong, I had shut myself off from the very things that make life meaningful?

Candice helped me see beyond my tough exterior to the person I had buried for so long. She didn't just teach me how to fight my way out of the chaos — she taught me how to embrace calm. With her guidance, I began to peel away the layers of armor I had built over the years. The journey was far from easy, but Candice walked with me, challenging me, guiding me, and showing me that true strength lies in surrendering, in finding the courage to be vulnerable, face your fears, and rebuild from within.

As a fighter, I thought I knew what it meant to be resilient. I thought strength was about how much I could endure. But Candice showed me that strength is also knowing when to stop fighting and start healing. She helped me understand that the battles we fight within ourselves are just as important as the ones we face outside. Healing isn't about fixing yourself — it's about allowing yourself to be seen, wounds and all. Every scar, every hurt, every moment I wanted to give up became part of my story, part of my journey toward peace.

The metaphor of the armor Candice writes about will resonate with anyone who has ever felt the need to protect themselves from the world. I was that person. I had spent years hiding behind a façade, convinced I didn't need help. Deep down, I was longing for someone to help me tear down the walls I had built around myself.

Candice didn't just help me break down my armor, she helped me understand why I had built it in the first place, and, more importantly, how to live without it. The journey wasn't easy. Some days, the healing process felt brutal, but Candice stood by me, guiding me back to myself.

This book offers a roadmap for anyone who is ready to move from chaos to calm. Candice's words aren't just for fighters like me, but for anyone who has ever felt weighed down by the burdens of the past. Her guidance is both practical and compassionate, offering hope to those ready to begin the journey of shedding their armor.

My transformation is ongoing. Like anyone on the path to healing, I still have moments where I feel the pull to retreat behind old patterns of protection. Fortunately, Candice has given me the tools to recognize those moments, face them with courage, and keep moving forward. She taught me that it's okay to be vulnerable, that real strength comes from letting go of control and allowing yourself to feel everything: the joy, the pain, and everything in between.

This book is not just a guide to healing — it's a guide to living. Candice speaks to the soul, gently reminding us that we are worthy of love, peace, and happiness, no matter how long we've carried our armor. If you're ready to stop fighting, to stop just surviving, and to start truly living, this book will be your companion on that journey. It's a journey I'm still on, and it's brought me closer to peace and closer to the person I was always meant to be.

Candice, thank you for seeing the person behind the boxer, for guiding me through my own darkness, and for helping me find my light.

— Margaret Sidoroff-Canty<br>
Champion Boxer,<br>
Coach, & Educator

# A Note to the Reader

This book is more than words on a page—it is an invitation to explore the layers of protection you've built over time and gently begin the process of uncovering what lies beneath. As you move through each chapter, I encourage you to keep a journal nearby. Use it to reflect on the lessons that resonate, to explore the emotions that arise, and to complete the guided activities at the end of each section.

For a deeper dive, you'll find a QR code at the end of each chapter leading to an expanded version of the activity. These exercises are designed to help you integrate what you've read into your daily life, making this journey not just one of understanding but of transformation.

Take your time. Be honest with yourself. And most importantly, approach this experience with curiosity and self-compassion.

With courage and surrender,
*Candice Knight*

# Introduction

*"The wound is the place where the light enters you." — Rumi*

Have you ever felt that you were moving through life wearing a suit of armor, protecting your heart from the world around you? For years, I wore mine without even knowing it.

Every day, millions of people wake up and put on an invisible suit of armor. This armor is not made of metal, but of past experiences, fears, and protective mechanisms we've developed over the years. We wear it to shield ourselves from emotional pain and vulnerability. But what if this armor is also preventing us from truly living, from experiencing the depth of connection and joy that life has to offer us?

I was at a friend's house, and I was tossing around some ideas with her about my book. She asked me a question that made me pause: "Who is your niche?" Instead of thinking of my target audience as a niche, I thought of them as 'my people.' I had considered 'my niche' before, but this was different. I wanted to give life to the people who might read my book so I wanted to make them real to me, not just some avatar for me to target.

A particular past client of mine came to mind. She had definitely had some hard knocks and had ended up becoming a professional fighter. Underneath her physical strength was a woman who would give immense time, energy, guidance, and care to anyone in need. At the same time, she loathed attention and would prefer to cheer from the sidelines, expecting absolutely nothing in return for her generosity. She told me that giving was her love language.

When I worked with her, I saw a wounded soul under the armor of a world-renowned boxer. We didn't seem to have much in common, yet our stories of struggle were interconnected in many ways. She got down to work and, even when the healing journey was brutal and she wanted to quit, she came back and dug a little deeper each time. She practiced the skills I taught her and applied them to all areas of her life. She revealed her darkness to me, and I helped her to turn it into her light. Although the process of removing her armor continues, as it does for all of us, she has stuck with it, making her an example of who my ideal person is.

My ideal person doesn't let any obstacle get them down or hold them back, at least not for long. No matter the challenges, the pain, or hopelessness, there is a spark inside that insists they get up, dust themselves off, and continue, more determined than ever. They may be motivated by feeling they have something to prove. The fact that they have convinced themselves that they don't need anyone or anything keeps them from being able to receive much more than the bare minimum of help.

Committed to not being a burden, they tend to overburden themselves with tasks, responsibilities, and unrealistic expectations. Although they have all the compassion in the world for everyone else, they show very little to themselves and are often their own worst enemy. The pursuit to improve and achieve is never-ending. Forced to mature at a young age, they often take on the role of nurturer and caregiver to anyone who needs support and a boost of confidence. They tend to see the best in everyone, even those who have shown their very worst time and time again.

This ideal person has a heart of gold, the bravery of a lion, and a soul that yearns for love, peace, and safety. They have finally reached the point where their armor has begun to crumble. Although they feel that they are falling apart, they are actually having a breakthrough. As usual, they refuse to give up. This time, however, they find themselves waking up, and they begin to remember. They might not have realized that their armor had begun to crack and crumble, falling away bit by bit, but now it is undeniable that something is happening and something needs to change. So accustomed to looking at what they must fix or change, when they look within, it becomes clear that it's time to stop, recalibrate, and release all that they have been clinging to for so long.

The weakness they feel ignites feelings of shame, guilt, and fear of losing control, of being seen, but the rebirth has begun and, although it's scary as heck, they have been through hell and back before so they get ready for a battle of a lifetime. They are ready to finally get out from under their confining armor and be free.

You might not resonate with everything I share in this book, but the principles are for anyone who has a few layers of armor to break free from. My hope is that you thoroughly read this book and see not only yourself, but also to realize that everyone is doing the best they can under the armor of their pain, hurt, and fears. Let this be a reminder to have compassion and to keep in mind that everyone has a story that they may not even be ready to share with themselves. If you are reading this book, then you ARE my ideal person. You are strong and soft all at the same time. You are brave, and you are finally ready to get back to the life you were always meant to lead. Welcome home!

This book is born out of a journey—a journey of breaking down, rebuilding, and learning to live authentically without the emotional armor that confined me.

In the pages that follow, we will delve into the concept of emotional armor. We'll explore its origins, how it manifests in our lives, and the impact it has on our relationships and self-perception. You'll read personal stories, both mine and others', that illustrate the power and perils of living behind a protective shield that cuts you off from a full life.

We'll also discuss practical strategies for recognizing and shedding this armor. From journaling and self-reflection, to seeking help and building supportive relationships, this book offers a roadmap for anyone ready to embark on the journey of self-discovery and healing.

This is not just a book about pain and over-protection. It's a guide to finding strength in vulnerability, to embracing our true selves, and to living a life of authenticity and connection. As you read, I hope you'll see that you're not alone. We all wear armor of some kind, but by acknowledging it and taking steps to shed its layers, we can open ourselves to deeper connections, greater self-compassion, and a more fulfilling life.

Before you begin, take a moment to try the **Shedding Your Armor Quiz**, and once you have finished reading the book, come back and see how your answers change.

Shedding Your Armor Quiz

# THE ARMOR WE WEAR
Exploring the Weight and Purpose of Our Emotional Armor

# Chapter 1
## Layers of Protection

*"The greatest glory in living lies not in never falling, but in rising every time we fall."*

— **Nelson Mandela**

According to American professor and author Brené Brown, "Whether we're fourteen or fifty-four, our armor and our masks are as individualized and unique as the personal vulnerability, discomfort, and pain we're trying to minimize."

Many people develop protective mechanisms to shield themselves from potential emotional pain. These protective behaviors manifest differently in each person, but the underlying principle is the same – it's a way to safeguard our emotional well-being.

Before I knew anything about the emotional armor I had been carrying, I hit rock bottom in 2013. Over about a year, my life transformed. So much so, I started a business and called it Phoenix Rising. I felt as if I had burnt down to ashes the life I had created for myself, and it was time for a rebirth. Little did I realize what would be involved in not only getting back on my feet, but also leaving the past behind.

At the time, I thought I was having a major mental and emotional breakdown. I remember being at work as a high school teacher and

# UNDER THE ARMOR

having to tell my principal that I couldn't return to the classroom following lunch. I had held back my feelings and experiences for so long, especially from people who barely knew me (and most definitely a superior at work) but on that day I just couldn't. I realized I had spent my whole life pushing through, getting things done and not asking for help, but it felt that I was crashing down and I needed help. I still wasn't ready to ask for it, but it was clear that I couldn't continue doing what I had always done.

I came to realize that **in our darkest moments, we actually have the greatest clarity to what our soul needs**. It is where the most significant healing journey begins. You don't have to hit rock bottom to start the healing process. You can make a choice and by reading this book, you are doing exactly that.

I was thirty-eight, and going through a rocky time in my marriage. My husband was studying nursing while working full time. I remember telling him I was scared. I felt that all the **cracks in our relationship were about to become a chasm, pulling us apart**. All the wounds we had patched up over the years were beginning to fester. I sensed the strain between us, and I knew we had to do something, but he was busy with other matters. The stress of his experiences was a lot for him to manage. Instead of bringing us close in partnership, it created a divide between us.

At the time our children were 6 and 8 years old, so I turned my attention to them and kept myself busy. At the same time I felt my marriage was shaken up, I had also become estranged from my family, and I had very few close friends. I started to keep everything to myself because whoever I reached out to couldn't or wouldn't support me the way I needed, although I can admit that I didn't know what I needed or how to ask for it. Every time I opened up and shared, I would be filled with feelings of guilt and shame. I felt the need to take care of it all on my own, but I truly couldn't.

The first place I turned to share what I was feeling was my journal, and that became a lifeline. I have journals that go back to the age of 12. Prior to writing this book, I looked through them, and I was both surprised and saddened by what I saw. There were clear patterns of my personality, my needs, my dislikes, and my pain.

My journals weren't just filled with times I felt alone, although it was definitely a way for me to release my feelings in a way that felt relatively safe. I probably censored myself in case someone read them. I think I held back from what I wanted to express because I didn't want to allow myself to be crass, negative, hateful, or angry. These omissions of my truth reflect how my armor put up guards because I had learned that I wasn't allowed to be angry. If I expressed how I truly felt, the result would be abandonment, so not even on paper in a journal meant for my eyes only did I allow myself the freedom to express myself.

During the dark days of my breakdown, my journals were a space to pour out my unfiltered thoughts, allowing me to confront and understand the complexities of my emotions. There is a particular journal filled with the most heinous words and statements directed toward myself and how much I hated who I had become. I am grateful that, when I came out of that period (which, thankfully, didn't last too long), I tore out the worst messages and burned them.

No matter what you might be feeling, journaling or any other form of creative expression can release emotions in a healthy manner. Sometimes it is the only healthy thing you are doing for yourself. If I had known then what I know now, I would have given myself permission to say it all, no matter how it might appear. Today, I have all the love, **compassion, and grace for every stage of myself reflected on those pages.** And here I am today, honestly, authentically, and vulnerably writing

this book.

What's interesting is that, even in some of my earliest journals, there are entries where I am writing to myself in a way that is comforting and supportive. Looking at those entries now, I can see that I was probably channeling messages from my guides, loved ones, or my higher self. When I had no one else to support me, I found it within myself.

For me, writing was a way to stop and reevaluate, take time for personal care, and have grace and compassion for myself, but at the beginning this was not easy. This was the battle between what I had learned and what I needed. This is when my armor began to crack open, but I didn't know what was happening except that I seemed to be losing all sense of control.

Eventually, I had to surrender and ask for help. I was dealing with a partner who seemed insensitive to my needs. On top of that, the family who had been my support over the years didn't want me in their life, so the people I would normally have turned to weren't there for me. This feeling of being utterly alone had happened before, but this seemed more significant. **I didn't know who to turn to — and that's when I found my way back to myself.**

The way I had handled situations before was not possible at that point. Previously, I had sucked it up and kept going. It felt that I had reached the tip of the mountain I had been climbing for as long as I could remember, and now I was crashing down with no one to save me. At the time, I felt so alone and unloved, but later I realized that being on my own ended up being exactly what I needed because that is when I began to turn to myself for guidance.

There was a time when all that kept me going each day was the love I had for my children. I told myself that they needed me to be strong, so I hid my tears until I could let those tears fall in the shower, my cries muffled by the running water. I don't really remember what triggered the shift, but eventually I had an awareness that I couldn't use my kids as my motivation. It wouldn't be fair to them if I were to rely solely on their love and dependence as the reasons to move forward. At some point, I realized how horribly I was treating myself, how miserable my life had become, and deep down there was a part of me saying I was worth so much more. It was a faint whisper, but once I heard it, it was something I tuned into to get me through to the greatest comeback of my life.

It took years of consistent effort to find my way to where I am today. My armor had begun to crack, but whenever I felt vulnerable and exposed, I did everything I could to patch up the spaces that were falling away. It took time, courage, and hope to help me let go of the only protection I had felt I could rely on. Along the way, strategies presented themselves that allowed me to embrace life feeling more prepared and equipped to handle whatever came my way.

I share principles with you later in the book, so that once you have become acquainted with your own unique armor and start to break free of it, you will be ready to practice the strategies that came to me when I needed help the most. In my darkest hours, there were glimpses of hope that ended up becoming my guiding principles.

If I had known about the armor I was carrying, it might have made the journey to where I am today smoother. Since it unfolded the way it did, I now have an opportunity to spare you the same struggle. Once you acknowledge the armor you wear, every step you make to become more self-aware will strip away the layers of weight, and you will feel more free and connected to your highest self.

We've explored the concept of emotional armor and how it can

# UNDER THE
# ARMOR

shield us from vulnerability. We've seen how hitting rock bottom can be a catalyst for profound change, and how even in our darkest moments, the seeds of healing can be found. Remember, you are not alone on this journey. We all wear armor of some kind. By acknowledging it and taking steps to shed its layers, we open ourselves to deeper connection, greater self-compassion, and a life lived more authentically.

My book is a roadmap to guide you. As you move forward, embrace the process. There will be setbacks, moments of doubt, and times when you want to retreat back into your armor. But with each step toward vulnerability, you'll experience growth and a renewed sense of self. So take a deep breath, shed a layer of your armor, and step into your power. You are worthy of love, connection, and a life filled with purpose. The greatest comeback of your life awaits you.

## TRY THIS:
Recognize and Address Your Emotional Armor

Take a moment to identify the protective mechanisms you've developed. Consider starting a journal where you can freely express your thoughts and emotions without self-censorship. This practice can help you begin to see and to acknowledge your emotional armor and begin the journey towards self-awareness and healing.

Activity 1

# Chapter 2:
## The Origins of Our Armor

*"I am not what happened to me, I am what I choose to become."*

— Carl Jung

Picture a suit of armor.

Does it resemble the clunky medieval kind, or a bulletproof vest worn by a police officer?

We all have an invisible shield we've crafted since our early days. It's our defense mechanism, shielding us from life's blows, shaping our responses, and often defining who we are. Where did this armor come from? Was it molded by childhood wounds, societal expectations, or the stories we've told ourselves over the years?

I remember speaking to my father before I left for Guatemala to attend the writing retreat where I began this book. I had reconnected with him a few months prior after no contact for close to four years. At the time of the call, I mentioned that I was about to write a book, and that became the focal point of our conversation.

I shared with him a few of my personal stories to help him make sense of the book's theme. My dad is well aware of how he contributed to my emotional armor, but I had long ago moved forward from the pain inflicted by him. I shared an example from my healing journey, and at the end, he said, "Just remember that you're a Knight."

His statement made me pause in shock and disbelief. It was as though I had heard my inherited birth name for the first time. I had already chosen the title of this book along with the image I wanted for the cover — a knight in armor that was cracking and starting to fall away, exposing rays of golden light from the soul about to be released. After assuming my partner's last name when we got married, I hadn't thought about my birth surname being Knight, for ages. It was at that moment I decided to change my name back to Knight so this book could be published under the name of the true warrior I had always been, but had lost sight of over the years.

My father was born in 1947 to two young immigrants of color from different countries, starting a new life together after surviving World War II. My grandad, from Barbados, fought on the front lines in Europe with the Canadian military, which is how he met my grandmother, a resident of Wales. They chose to start their family in Canada, which was a land of opportunity and a place for a fresh start.

My grandfather brought with him PTSD from his time as a soldier. Together, they brought not only their belongings, but also the baggage of their past. I am sure they were excited, but mixed with the exhilaration of new love and freedom, there was also the anxiety of creating a home without the support of family or friends. This only got more complicated when my grandmother found out she had tuberculosis while pregnant with my father.

She had to move from the home she had just begun to feel settled in, and was quarantined in a sanitorium. When she gave birth to her first born child, my father, he was immediately whisked away to prevent him from getting sick as well. My grandfather, who worked during the

# UNDER THE ARMOR

day, had my father placed in the care of a family and would pick him up each night. My dad did not reunite with his mother until he was three years old. I can't begin to imagine what that was like for all of them or the residual armor this experience created.

I remember looking at a picture of my dad taken when he was about six months old and my telling him that was probably how far back he needed to go in order to heal the layers of his own armor. When I think of constructing my own, I find myself going back to a time I can't even recall — the age of two. At that age, my sister was born with immense health problems, and like most firstborn children, I learned that I was no longer the top priority.

A big part of my emotional armor goes back to believing I had only myself to rely on. I probably created a narrative to comfort myself and keep myself in line. My mom and other loving adults would have done their best to give me the love I wanted, but I wonder what I might have done to get more of it. I imagine I began to crave being seen, but held back to avoid being a bother, and this shows up to this day.

Imagine getting praised for being a good girl by staying out of the way, not expressing feelings, and not burdening anyone with your needs or wants. Many of you probably silenced yourself to avoid discipline or to earn praise. When you needed love and attention, you learned to give it to yourself, because you didn't want to seem selfish or an inconvenience. So you tucked it all away behind the armor that formed to protect your tender, feeling heart.

That conversation with my father was a profound revelation. His reminder that I was a Knight became exactly what I needed to see the depth of meaning in what I was about to do. Beyond writing a book, I was reclaiming my birth name, symbolizing shedding the armor that concealed my true warrior spirit. **My father, for better or worse, had**

**made me a Knight in the first place.** No wonder I had no difficulty changing it when I got married. I had never felt connected to it or to my father. Choosing to be a knight, armor-free, sheds light on the universal struggle to dismantle protective barriers and embrace the shared vulnerability that binds us all.

Like me, you might be unable to pinpoint the exact events that triggered your emotional armor. Even if you think you know, you might doubt that something so long ago could have a lasting impact. Maybe you resist this trip down memory lane because it's painful, or you might not want to seem like you are placing blame. Some memories are difficult to examine, but these experiences, tucked away under your armor, thrive without you being aware. **When you dare to look back, you have the opportunity to heal the root of what creates chaos in your life today.** Too often, we treat the surface symptoms, but by turning inward we get to the source, and the real healing can begin.

We've delved into the concept of emotional armor, exploring how it forms in response to life's experiences, often from a young age. This armor protects us, but it can limit our capacity for connection and growth. The journey to healing isn't about pinpointing blame or dwelling on the past. It's about acknowledging our armor's presence and understanding its origins. By recognizing the stories we tell ourselves and the patterns established in childhood, we can dismantle the layers that no longer serve us.

This process may involve revisiting uncomfortable memories, but the reward is immense. By shedding our armor, we reconnect with our authentic self, the warrior within, ready to face life's challenges with courage and vulnerability. Your willingness to heal empowers you and paves the way for future generations to experience healthier dynamics. The cycle of trauma repeats until someone decides to end it and prevent the next generation from being affected.

# UNDER THE
# ARMOR

As you explore your past, celebrate the moments of love and support you received. Acknowledge the challenges and begin healing the wounds that shaped your armor. This is an ongoing process, but with each layer shed, you'll experience a renewed sense of freedom and connection. You are strong, capable of immense strength and vulnerability. Embrace both, and step into the life you were always meant to live.

## TRY THIS:
Uncover and Heal the Roots of Your Emotional Armor

Reflect on the early experiences and relationships that shaped your emotional defenses. Consider speaking with family members or revisiting childhood memories to gain insights. This awareness can help you dismantle your armor and reconnect with your authentic self. Journaling about these reflections can be a powerful first step in your healing journey.

Activity #2

# Chapter 3:
## The Influence of Early Experiences

*"Out of suffering have emerged the strongest souls; the most massive characters are seared with scars."*

— **Kahlil Gibran**

There are subtle cues that betray the presence of our emotional armor.

Have you ever questioned the signals indicating your instinctive defense mechanisms have been triggered? They tend to creep up unexpectedly, yet in some instances, they show up like clockwork in our daily lives. These are indicators that point to how we shield our truest selves. Some of us are fidgety while we wait, or avoid eye contact when we feel especially vulnerable. There are also those seemingly harmless habits, such as planning every detail or being busy all the time. These are just a few of the telltale signs of our emotional armor that often go unnoticed.

On January 1, 1990, just 8 days before my 15th birthday, my life changed forever. It was the first day of a new decade, and my mom was taking my Oma, her mother, back home. My brother and I were going to stay with Oma for the remainder of the Christmas holidays because my mom had to return to work. This was the first year my Oma had ever spent Christmas with us. My Opa, her husband, had died almost

# UNDER THE ARMOR

two years prior, so family traditions had begun to change. I remember that Thanksgiving, as my Oma had told people she had put their names on the items she wanted them to have once she died. My uncle chided her, saying she wasn't going to die any time soon.

While she was at our home for the holidays, she came to me with a box that held a charm bracelet inside. On the inside cover of the box, she had inscribed a message of love. When she handed it to me, she told me that she was going to leave this for me when she died, but decided to give it to me now. Just like I had heard my uncle say, at what would be the final family get-together, I reassured her that she wouldn't die any time soon. Yet she died just days later, along with my mother and my brother.

We were driving down a country highway, and at one point my mom went off the concrete road and onto the gravel-lined shoulder. When she corrected and turned the wheels to get back on the road, the car began to spin on a patch of black ice. The car turned into oncoming traffic and was hit on the passenger's side. Our small Chevrolet Citation was totaled, so much so that the rescuers had to use a crowbar-like device called 'the jaws of life' to extract me from the vehicle. My mom and grandmother died instantly, and my brother and I were rushed to the hospital, where he was taken off life support soon after.

To this day, I have no memory of anything that happened that day, but early on, I did have some haunting thoughts associated with the crash. The smell of blood, the piercing sound of my Oma screaming my mother's name before the impact, and then nothing until I was in the hospital, recovering. I have no memory of the man who tried to save my life, the doctor who stabilized me, the surgery, or my uncle telling me what had happened. My armor was protecting me from a horror no one should ever have to recall, and I am so thankful for that.

The hospital I recovered in was directly across the street from my high school in Oshawa, Ontario, Canada. I remained in traction to stabilize my shattered femur for a month and a half, in a room with windows that refused to open and offer a reprieve from the stale air. I found myself at the crossroads of vulnerability and resilience.

Exams loomed, and the weight of responsibility pressed down on me. The goal, of course, was to recover from a near-fatal accident and the heartbreaking loss of those closest to me, but I added other pressures to myself. I didn't want to fail. I didn't want to be seen as someone who needed special treatment. Deep down, I may have already begun to fear that if I didn't prove my worth and resilience, I wouldn't be wanted by the family I was set to live with.

There might have been an underlying panic, yet a stoic calm prevailed, for the most part. The conflict was that a part of me felt that I needed to be sad and break down through my grief, but another part was resolved to get things done, not be a burden, and not fail by any standards. I may have also felt trapped. I couldn't go anywhere. I had no real control over who would visit me, going to the bathroom in privacy was a luxury, I couldn't open the window for fresh air, and I didn't have a choice as to where I would live once I was released.

With my high school directly across the street, I probably felt that as much as I wanted the support of my friends, I also couldn't say no to having them visit. They were a distraction to me, I suppose, yet to them I may have been an oddity and wonder. I may have felt this with everyone, family included. Even if I had wanted to break down and cry, I didn't have the privacy. I had to share my room with at least one other patient, and since I couldn't get out of bed, I was never alone. Can you see how this set me up to hold my emotions in, tucked away, safely under my armor?

# UNDER THE ARMOR

Not long ago, I had an intuitive reading with someone, and they told me that it was no wonder I still struggled to recover. The day of the accident, I had been given the gift of life, so how could I possibly feel that I deserved anything more? I mention this because the journey isn't just about physical and emotional healing related to an event that is easy to pinpoint. **The journey is a lifetime, as different facets of healing are triggered and require attention.** Once you are aware and willing to accept that there are still remnants to be attended to, you will continue to move forward.

There are, no doubt, many signs that someone is presenting their best selves from behind a shield. I presented so many simply during the time I was in the hospital because that's how I had already learned to cope with trauma. Who knew I'd already be prepared to deal with this life-altering tragedy? I wrote my exams in the hospital, even though I was told I didn't need to. I told myself I didn't want to fail and didn't want special treatment. When asked by a classmate why I wasn't crying, I responded by telling him that all the crying in the world would never bring them back.

As I processed my grief and the guilt I had for being the sole survivor, I convinced myself that it was me that had to survive. If it had been my mom, she would have felt she had killed her mother and two of her three children. My Oma would have dealt with the grief of losing her only daughter and two grandchildren, plus she had just lost her husband two years prior. My 10-year- old brother would have had to live with my father, which would have been horrible for him.

It wasn't until after my breakdown in 2013, that I considered the idea of a soul's journey. Even though I wasn't aware of this concept at the time of the accident, my Oma letting everyone know her plans for her belongings following her death and my belief that out of all of us, I was the one meant to live, shows that I had some understanding of something greater than myself even back then. Imagine feeling this way, but not feeling safe enough to share this with anyone else. I kept the spiritual impact of this experience closely guarded to protect myself. I couldn't bear the idea of anyone telling me I was wrong, because my beliefs were all I had.

Despite the reality I faced, some very spiritual things happened which may have ignited my belief that everything happens for a reason. The mention of spirit, the universe, my higher self, or any other spiritual reference is inevitable. For me, there has been no deeper healing than when I connected with something beyond my conscious thoughts and experiences.

An example of that is related to my brother. I couldn't speak about Adam without crying. He had been sitting beside me in the backseat of the car. Even though I couldn't remember the accident, the event was etched in my subconscious mind. One night, I had a dream/vision about him letting me know that he was okay. He told me that even though he didn't want to leave me, he had to go with mom because if he stayed he would never have been the boy he was before the accident. He was the only person who didn't die instantly, but he had been declared brain dead, and the family had chosen to take him off life support. He was already gone by the time I had this vision, but it allowed me to talk about him again and be okay with the fact that I was here and he wasn't, or just that he was gone at all.

Why soldier on? It wasn't just about exams or keeping up appearances; it was a deeper fear – the fear of being perceived as someone who couldn't handle life, who needed special treatment, or who might not be wanted. There may have also been the fear that I would lose myself in grief and not be able to move forward. The struggle was real, but so was the determination not to falter. I didn't want to be a burden and, if you know anything about the body-mind connection, it is interesting

# UNDER THE
# ARMOR

that I had shattered my right femur, the largest bone in the entire human body on the side focused on getting things done. No matter what, I was forced to rest, heal, and be cared for.

Today, I can articulate my belief that **we are all on a soul's journey** and before we came into our current life, we decided to live our lives with all the ups and downs we have experienced and will continue to experience. I imagine that, as a soul, I agreed to have an abusive father, to be the sole survivor of a car crash, to be a biracial female born in Canada as a member of generation X. My mother's soul agreed to her experiences, my father his, my sister and brother theirs. I chose my husband to help me heal my karmic wounds, and my children, by choosing us as their guides, will have lessons to learn and heal from as well.

I can see the balance between vulnerability and resilience during my hospital stay, and it becomes evident that emotional armor is both a shield and a survival mechanism. My journey through tragedy is an example of the layers we construct to navigate life's complexities.

When I was finally discharged from the hospital, I was physically on the mend, but I remained emotionally fragile. It took decades even to know that I was protecting the most delicate part of myself and, because I was unaware, I had added on a number of additional layers of armor. The choices I made throughout life were influenced by this armor and made my healing journey complex, time-consuming, and at times I thought it would be impossible for me to feel whole. The subtle signs of emotional armor, explored in this journey, serve as a reminder of the strength within us all that arises when it seems that all we can do is survive.

As you look at how coping mechanisms indicate a need for self-preservation, a pattern will be revealed. We like to imagine that we are complicated individuals, but when you come down to it, there are core needs that motivate us to either move forward or retreat. We might even convince ourselves that what we are doing represents our strength, independence, and capabilities, but what we fail to acknowledge is that what we have been telling ourselves for so long is just another layer of armor trying to keep us from being hurt. How does your behavior keep you armored, anxious, and feeling all alone?

We've embarked on a journey to understand the complexities of emotional armor. We've explored the subtle signs – the fidgeting, the busyness, the stoicism – all defense mechanisms that shield us during times of vulnerability. These shields have served a purpose. They have protected us from the harsh realities of life, especially after experiencing profound loss. But as we've seen through my story, the accident wasn't just a physical trauma — it fractured my sense of self-worth and shattered my world.

The beauty lies in the human spirit's unwavering strength. Even armored, I pushed forward and faced the world with determined resilience. This strength is a testament to the warrior that resides within each of us. Now, with time and awareness, comes the opportunity to shed the layers of armor I no longer need. This process isn't about self-criticism — it's about acknowledging the presence of our emotional armor and honoring the role it plays in our survival.

As we peel back these layers, we reconnect with our vulnerability, the very essence of our authentic selves. This vulnerability isn't weakness — it's the wellspring of connection, empathy, and genuine human connection. By sharing my story, I hope to inspire others to explore their own protective layers. Let us shed the armor together, not in a show of weakness, but in a celebration of our shared humanity. As we step into the world, vulnerable and strong, we embrace the beautiful messiness of life, ready to connect with ourselves and others on a deeper level.

# UNDER THE ARMOR

## TRY THIS:
### Identify Your Emotional Armor

Pay attention to subtle cues in your behavior, such as fidgeting, avoiding eye contact, or being overly busy. These may be signs of your emotional armor. Take a moment to reflect on these habits and consider journaling about when and why they arise. This awareness can help you understand and start to dismantle your protective layers, allowing your true self to emerge.

Activity #3

# CANDICE KNIGHT

# PART 2

## CRACKS IN OUR ARMOR
Recognizing and Acknowledging Our Vulnerability

# Chapter 4:
## Recognizing Our Armor

---

*"Our scars can destroy us,
even after the physical wounds have healed.
But if we allow them to,
they can transform us into something greater."*

## — Alice Miller

The core idea here is that emotional armor, though seemingly protective, remains a constant companion, shielding us from our earliest and deepest wounds. As I share my story, you will accompany me through the decades of my life, understanding how my armor, crafted at the tender age of two, persisted in shielding the same wound. The echo remained that I was not secure and had only myself to rely on.

I believe that when I was two years old, after my sister's birth, her health challenges became the catalyst for the construction of my emotional armor. In addition, my parents' troubled marriage motivated me to adopt the role of a good child, steering clear of any trouble, and doing my best as a toddler not to be a bother. The notion that my parents had something more important to focus on than my needs planted the seed of insecurity, as well as the belief that I needed to be a certain way to receive the attention I craved from the people I cared about.

Of course, I have no recollection of being two years old, but I can

# UNDER THE
# ARMOR

imagine that any firstborn child faces some challenges adapting to a new baby in the home. As a toddler, our level of comprehension that we now must share our parents' attention with someone else would no doubt be a tantrum trigger. It might seem silly to imagine that this is when my armor began to be constructed, but the point here is for you to see that **your own armor probably began before you ever knew you needed a buffer at all**.

By age 7, my armor solidified as my father, a physically abusive alcoholic, endangered my mother's life. My frantic attempts to intervene reinforced my lack of security, power, and protection. Now, not only was I unshielded, but my mom became another person I felt I had to defend. By losing control, the one who should protect me most, my father, showed a complete disregard for my well-being. Did my parents tumultuous relationship foreshadow how a future man I loved and trusted would treat me?

Following the tragic car accident, I went to live with my mom's brother and his family. In my journals, I wrote of how grateful I was, but I ended up feeling that I was a burden more than anything else. Any attempts I made to effectively earn my place often went unacknowledged or left me feeling that no matter what I did, it would never be enough to be viewed as valuable and worth keeping. Contemplating self-harm, I withdrew into my bedroom to seek solace in music, writing, and memories.

I always feared that I would be kicked out of the home if I dared to express my true feelings, and I believed that everyone would be happier and better off if I weren't around. This difficult time surpassed the challenges of my mother's death, leaving me feeling alone and pressured to embody perfection to remain where I was. Keeping myself away from the family was, in itself, an example of armor. I created a protective space, not because there was any danger of harm, but because I felt so insignificant that the cocoon-like sanctuary of my room provided me a place to express myself and be alone with my thoughts.

From the ages of 15-17, it wasn't just the adjustment to creating a life without my loved ones — it was also acclimating myself to yet another new school, this one with its own set of challenges, and managing the angst that comes with simply being a teen, all the while doing my best to be inconspicuous. No matter what I was feeling, I did what any well-adjusted young person would do — I balanced my classes with school group involvement, spent time with my friends, and held a part-time job. I truly did my best to be a teen any adult could be proud of, yet I always felt that it was never enough, so I worked through my conflicting emotions in my journals and tried to hold it all together, even though everything seemed to be falling apart.

In the midst of eleventh grade, I reached out to my dad's sister living in the Toronto area and asked if I could spend the summer with her and her family. I figured that everyone in the home I was currently living in needed a break, including myself. Before long, that summer break plan turned into a plea to move in for my final year of high school. In the end, weeks prior to the end of the school year, my aunt told me to get out of the house, which left me to finish the remainder of my classes living with another brother of my mom's, who, thankfully, lived close to my high school. Despite the stress of this whole situation, my armor aided me in holding things together, and I had no doubt that better things were on the horizon.

In my 20s, I rebelled by immersing myself in pursuing higher education, seeking distance from my family to avoid the sting of being unwanted. I chose to move to Windsor, Ontario, because it was about 3 hours from my family, which would ensure that I would be even less of a burden and at the same time I might not feel the sting of being unwanted since I was so far away and could tell myself that was the reason

# UNDER THE
# ARMOR

I didn't get to see family very often. When it did come time for a visit, the old adage "absence makes the heart grow fonder" seemed applicable. For a moment, I would feel missed, loved, and, in a way, I felt that I belonged.

One of the protective aspects of my armor was to lose myself in these moments because for a time, at least, I felt loved. I was loved. I know that to be true as much as I know that everyone who had me in their care did the best they could for me. The burden I put on myself, though, was to use that belief as a way to excuse the lack of love and support that I needed. Even if they did what they could, loved me as much as they were able, and tried their best to include me as a part of their family, I wasn't. They knew it and I felt it, yet, because I didn't feel safe to share those feelings, I tucked them away under my armor and got myself a distance away to make everyone feel more comfortable.

Academic achievement became my shield, a subconscious attempt to prove my worth to those who were seemingly indifferent to my achievements. Part of me earned degree after degree to prove my worth to those who never seemed to care what I did, as long as it didn't make them look bad or require anything from them. The other part of me got three degrees and a diploma to create what I thought would lead to security — financial security, to be exact. The pursuit of financial security masked the deeper fear that "no one cared about me," so I would always have to make sure I had the means to provide for myself.

Just as I was entering my 30s, the desire for love and family led me to marriage. Initially blissful, the union unraveled following the birth of our second child, revealing that I had unwittingly married my wounds. Despite clear signs, I clung to the belief that we were meant to be and sought the security and care that had remained elusive the majority of my life. By the time I had married, my mother had been dead for half my life. The choices I was making went deeper than that loss, though, as the wounds related to love, rejection, and abandonment went back to the beginning, even though I wasn't aware of that at all. I was also unaware of how deep the pain went of feeling rejected and abandoned by the people who stepped in to care for me after my mom died. My mom didn't "choose" to leave me, but so many others chose not to have me in their life. It just reaffirmed that I was not wanted, which made me abandon myself even further.

In my mid 40s, the gift of my husband ending our marriage became the wake-up call I had needed for years. I had already been here before. Not only had I previously been able to provide security for myself and my children, I had also had some practice of allowing people to let go of me without me feeling the need to try harder to hold on. The interesting thing is that just a couple of months after my husband left, Covid shut the world down, including the border with America which, for a year and a half, allowed my children and me to create our new normal without the influence of the discomfort of the separation. It was almost as though layers of armor were removed without me having to do anything at all. I quickly realized that what I had worried about the most, being on my own, having to do everything by myself, was actually a blessing that I didn't see until that became my reality.

The next phase of healing involved trusting myself not to try to find someone to help me figure out this new life. Mind you, I did have to ask for help every now and then from my friends and neighbors, but it was different. Whenever I thought about what my ex would do if we were still married, I would reflect back on what it was like when he was in fact living in the house. The reality was that I would make most of the decisions, pay the majority of the costs, and figure out most challenges on my own. It wasn't just because my ex wouldn't help out, I know now, but that I never knew how to let him take care of things because of the doubts, fears, and beliefs my armor had led me to believe all this time.

# UNDER THE
# ARMOR

When I was feeling particularly sorry for myself, I would ask myself what it would look like if he just wasn't around at all. When I resented him or wished that he would do more to help me out, it would make me miserable. I have always hated feeling sorry for myself — I was uncomfortable with anger and, in the end, I figured these emotions wouldn't get me anywhere. I did what I had gotten really good at doing — I assessed the situation, made a plan, and did what needed to be done. As I mentioned before, it was only after I started writing this book that it came to me that actually looking at those less than positive feelings is essential to healing. In the meantime, my strategy served me well, and I can thank my gilded emotional armor for that.

For so long, the obstacle lay in holding onto the hurt from my early years, preserving myself in a world where guidance through love was absent. Always seeking validation from external sources, explaining myself to be understood, and withholding true feelings became the norm. Yet, through all scenarios, I hunkered down, achieved, and persevered, always trying to prove my worth. Success in every endeavor was my shield, fueled by an innate belief that destiny awaited me. When I finally realized that pushing through keeps you from healing, I was able to look at myself with gentle compassion, and it was shocking to imagine how much I was carrying that didn't belong to me now — or ever.

It is daunting to take a trip down memory lane when it is the memories that you are trying to stifle behind the armor you wear. As a warrior, feeling sorry for yourself or, worse yet, having someone pity you, is not an option. You hunker down with the bare necessities, and find a way to persevere through anything that comes your way. You also convince yourself that you don't need help from anyone unless absolutely necessary and, whatever you take, you give back tenfold someway, somehow. You don't want to owe anyone anything, you don't want to be perceived as weak or ungrateful and, even though you want more than anything to be loved, nurtured, and to have a safe space to be yourself, you feel safer sharing only a small part of yourself and keeping your guard up.

Once you take a trip through the memories of your own life journey, you will see all the times you had to armor up as a way to protect your body, mind, heart, and soul. It is not for the faint of heart, but you have made it this far, and you're ready to lay down the sword, whatever it looks like for you. How many layers of armor have you accumulated over the years, and how many layers of other people's baggage are you carrying as your own? Put it down so that you are free to get to the heart of the matter. The heart of everything you need to heal lies beneath your armor.

Your story is a testament to your enduring spirit. You've carried a heavy load, an emotional armor forged in the fires of early childhood experiences. This armor served its purpose – it shielded you from a world that felt unsafe, offering a sense of control amidst the chaos. But as you've bravely delved into your past, a profound truth emerges: true healing requires vulnerability. The "warrior" you've become isn't just about stoic resilience — it's about acknowledging and processing the pain you've carried for so long.

This journey of self-discovery isn't about discarding the armor entirely. Perhaps some pieces still serve a purpose, offering a sense of groundedness during moments of vulnerability. But it's about learning to choose when to wear the armor and when to lay it down. It's about understanding that beneath the layers of protection lies tender emotion – the very essence of your authentic self. It's about allowing yourself to feel the full spectrum, the joy and the sorrow, the strength and the vulnerability.

This is the call to action for all who carry their own armor. Explore

# UNDER THE
# ARMOR

your history, confront the hurts you've held onto, and shed the layers that no longer serve you. Embrace your vulnerability, not as weakness, but as the key to authentic connection and compassion. Remember, the warrior isn't defined by the armor they wear, but by the courage to face themselves and the world with an open heart. This is where your true strength lies, in embracing your whole self, wounds and all. As you embark on this path, know that you are not alone. We are all warriors on this journey of self-discovery, and together we can shed our armor and embrace the beauty of our shared humanity.

## TRY THIS:
### Create a Timeline of Key Events

Reflect on significant moments in your life that contributed to the formation of your emotional armor. Create a timeline, starting with your earliest memories, and note the key events where you felt the need to protect yourself. Consider how these experiences shaped your beliefs and behaviors. By identifying these pivotal moments, you can begin to release the layers of protection that no longer serve you, allowing for a more authentic and connected self.

Activity #4

# Chapter 5:
## The Purpose of Our Armor

*"Trauma is not what happens to you.
Trauma is what happens inside you
as a result of what happened to you."*

### — Gabor Maté

The car accident I survived as a teen left me with not only severe physical injuries requiring a protective layer to heal, but also a tender heart in need of emotional armor to ward off haunting memories. As life unfolded post-collision, these emotional shields became my refuge. The years following the crash presented many challenges, causing me to rely on my armor time and again, creating a layered effect—pain building on pain. It wasn't until much later, during a profound meditation, that I confronted the unseen battleground within.

In 2022, I stumbled upon what repression looked like within me, and it was monumental. We all harbor aspects of our past that we wish to forget, and, like me, some experience trauma-induced amnesia, a subconscious act of self-preservation. We might only become aware of the complexities of our emotional armor when we directly confront what it is we are avoiding, which we put off to avoid the pain waiting to be healed. We realize the shields we carry when circumstances require us to face what they have been protecting us from.

# UNDER THE
# ARMOR

Sigmund Freud, the founder of psychoanalysis, is well-known for his beliefs surrounding a person's reliance on defense mechanisms as a way to cope with challenges. His belief was that the mind buries distressing thoughts into the unconscious to protect the individual from overwhelming anxiety. My initial lack of awareness of what I was repressing mirrors Freud's notion that these defense mechanisms often operate unconsciously.

Although the actual event was buried in my subconscious memory, the car accident was a pivotal moment for my life in many ways. The collision, the wreckage, the lives lost—my body trapped, my femur shattered, and my consciousness fully intact was a brush with mortality that left an indelible mark. Only recently did I realize that this gift of life might have left me with feelings of undeservingness, found in survivor's guilt, and could have had me questioning whether I deserved more in life when I was the sole survivor of a car accident that claimed everyone else.

Fast forward to a transformative moment at a Mindvalley University event during the summer of 2022. During an inner child meditation, a suppressed aspect of myself emerged—an embodiment of everything I had ever repressed so that I could continue on. This version of myself was resentful, unattractive, and bore the weight of all my suppressed trauma. Not only that, but she had been the bearer of my anger, resentment, frustration, and victimhood for the entirety of my life.

It was during this poignant meditation that I faced the heart-wrenching realization that I had never even considered this part of myself before. What I had always done was referred to this aspect as my ugly self, which dismissed the part of me that encapsulated vulnerability, authenticity, pain, and the need to be seen, heard, and loved. Tears streamed down my face as I apologized, finally recognizing the depth of her sacrifice. **This dark shadow held the stories I dared not**

# CANDICE KNIGHT

share, the truths I repressed to shield others from the raw, exposed me.

She was hunched over and black, as though covered in soot, yet she was undoubtedly me. She turned to me with a snarl on her deformed face. She had a bone to pick. She told me that I had called her ugly, and she was livid. She confronted me, challenging my perception of resilience. She was the unsung hero, the one who had taken on the emotional burden to ensure my survival through life's relentless trials.

How did I think I got through all the things I experienced? How did I think I was able to write those exams and keep going? Three degrees and a diploma?? She listed a bunch of other experiences of trauma and how I had managed to plow through. She said that it was all because of her! She had been my subconscious dumping ground. She ridiculed me for thinking it was because I was a firstborn, type A Capricorn. It was because she took all the difficulties so that I didn't have to stop. How was I still alive when I had contemplated suicide time and again??? Her. It was all her.

I hadn't known that, and I told her so. She turned away from me, her fierceness subdued. I went to her and brushed the dust off of her, telling her over and over again how sorry I was. I told her that I didn't know about her. She reminded me, in a broken voice, of all the times I had called her ugly. I had, but I didn't mean it like that. Even though I didn't know about her, I had referred to her as the part of all of us that we rarely let others see, that "ugly" part, when we are real, raw, and exposed. I thought I was protecting those parts, those stories, but **I was repressing my truth to protect others from — me.**

This was heartbreaking. I remember the tears streaming from my eyes during the meditation. I recall holding my breath and tightening my lips, trying with all my might to hold it all in. As usual, I didn't want

# UNDER THE
# ARMOR

anyone to see me break down, even though others in attendance were wailing all over the room, having their own emotional breakthroughs. I then felt a gentle touch at the top of my head from one of the "angels" or assistants for the meditation, and with that brief gesture of kindness, I cried, and cried, and cried.

When I was done weeping, I recall the facilitator telling us to release or let go of whatever had come up. My soul aspect, now standing straighter, less hardened and less hideous, turned to me and said she wasn't going anywhere. Although she looked 14, probably the time she took on the biggest burden of all, she had been with me from the start and would be with me until the very end. She was a vital part of me. She asked me to never refer to her as ugly and to never forget she was there or how much she loved me. Isn't that why she had carried all those burdens for me in the first place? She loved me so much that she chose to suffer so I didn't, or at least not as much as I might have.

This revelation made the abstract notion of subconscious suppression that Freud has shared with the world personal to me and paved the way for deeper healing that I wasn't aware I needed. My inner child's plea was a wake-up call and reminder that I needed to finally acknowledge and embrace the part of myself that I had repressed for so long in a manner that I had yearned for from others in my life. For so long my focus had been on basic survival, but it was now time for me to prepare to thrive in life, not just get by. Although I had come out of the accident physically better off in comparison to everyone else, my emotional well-being was linked to how effectively I pleased those in charge of my care. Their satisfaction took precedence over my personal flourishing and even my human right to make mistakes and grow from them. This perception remained with me and created a layer of armor that took repeated wake-up calls to release.

It still took another year, after I was introduced to my shadow aspect, before I was able to consciously look at how suppressing my darker emotions had impacted my life. Those burdens had become my limiting beliefs, and each one was tied to the lies I had come to believe about my value and worth. They had kept me rooted in the past, anchoring me to fear and doubt. Until I fully acknowledged these beliefs that negated every affirmation I had ever claimed, all my desires would remain under a self-imposed glass ceiling, so close, so visible, yet always beyond my reach.

Surviving the tragic car accident required not just physical resilience, but a profound psychological suppression, allowing me to navigate life's aftermath. Unearthing the part of me that bore the brunt of this trauma was unsettling. The journey from repression to acknowledgment was pivotal. When I was younger and had just suffered the greatest loss of my life, it had fueled my will to keep going.

As an adult, consciously focused on healing, the awareness of what I had done to myself became the catalyst for self-acceptance and integration. No longer did I need to fragment myself for the sake of others. No longer did I need to worry about the feelings of others to the suppression of my own. This realization marked a significant milestone in my quest to embrace the full spectrum of my being, shadows and all.

You might be ready to take a look at your layers of armor, and in some ways the reason why you have had to protect your vulnerable nature is obvious. What is less clear is how it affected you on a deeper, subconscious level, and once you open yourself up to that awareness, it can be challenging. Your truth is nothing you can't handle, but you may need support as you explore the various sides of yourself. For so many of us, this is the most difficult thing to receive. The process is yours alone to navigate, but you never need to do it alone. Realizing that is part of your healing, and a layer of armor removed.

# UNDER THE ARMOR

The car accident fractured not just my bones, but my sense of self. The layers of emotional armor I constructed served a purpose – they protected a wounded soul navigating a world forever altered. However, during my transformative meditation, the truth emerged, embodied in the form of the "ugly" aspect I'd long repressed.

This revelation was a punch to the gut, yet a necessary one. It forced me to confront how I'd demonized a part of myself that carried my burdens, allowing me to survive. The anger, resentment, and pain were not ugliness, but a reflection of the trauma I'd endured and an indicator of what I needed to acknowledge and heal.

This awakening ignited a journey of self-acceptance. I apologized to this neglected part of my consciousness, vowing to acknowledge her as a vital piece of my being. Integration, not suppression, became the key. This inner work wasn't easy. It meant confronting the limiting beliefs formed in the wake of trauma, and the self-doubt that held me captive. With each layer peeled back, a more authentic self emerged.

The accident may have required physical armor, but true healing demanded emotional vulnerability. Now I embrace the full spectrum of my being – the light and the shadow. This journey is a testament to the human spirit's ability to heal, to transform even the deepest wounds into self-compassion and wholeness.

Your story, too, can be one of self-discovery. Perhaps you've built similar emotional armor to shield a vulnerable core. Remember, the truth you seek is within you, waiting to be acknowledged. It may be challenging, but it's a journey worth taking. By embracing our vulnerabilities, we shed the layers of armor and step into the world authentically. This is where genuine connection flourishes, where we connect not just with others, but with the most important person of all: ourselves.

## TRY THIS:
Confront Your Emotional Armor

Spend some quiet time in meditation or reflection to identify any parts of yourself you've been suppressing. Write down these feelings and consider how they've protected you but also limited your growth. Acknowledge and thank these aspects, and begin the process of integrating them into your whole self. This practice can help you embrace vulnerability and foster deeper self-acceptance.

Activity #5

# Chapter 6:
## The Armor Between Us

---

*"Your task is not to seek for love,*
*but merely to seek and find all the barriers within yourself*
*that you have built against it."*

### — **Rumi**

The armor we wear becomes most evident in our connections with other people. Our relationships are where we hope to feel safe enough to be unguarded, yet the armor of past traumas directs every action to become either a call for love or an act of love, rooted in the profound urge for acceptance and belonging.

An act of love is anything we do when our heart is free to be fully expressed. We give, we laugh, we share without fear or expectations. This is our natural state of being.

A call for love doesn't have to be a negative experience, unless our armor interferes with the transmission from our hearts to another person's ears. When my call for love feels unheard or rejected, I find myself shifting between a muted voice and a roaring cry. Both responses will inevitably be misunderstood and can potentially push people away. The balance between giving and receiving love becomes a tightrope walk. When I doubted that I deserved what I desired, I often hesitated to say anything at all. I thought that holding back would keep me from being disappointed, but, in the end, it made my call for love misunderstood, which led to even more frustration for everyone involved.

Unbeknownst to me, this armor was shaping my reality. It wasn't the people around me, but the reflection of my beliefs about myself that influenced how I showed up in relationships. It was the way I showed up, presented myself, communicated, reacted, and, in the end, my relationships became exactly as I expected them to be, not as I wanted them to be. Clearly, our expectations create our reality. **Despite what we think we desire, we attract what we believe we are worth.**

I avoided challenging someone because the truth is that I feared the response or feedback I might receive, knowing it might hurt. Beneath this fear is the limiting belief that my feelings are not as valid as someone else's and that any possibility of wrongdoing on my part equated to me somehow being a "bad" person. Instead of revealing that the person had any power over me and my emotions, I would just be quiet, laugh off any hurtful comments, and retreat to a place of solitude as soon as I could. Where I believed my armor was protecting me, this resistance to expressing myself was actually doing more harm than good.

I have always known that not everyone is going to like me, but that never stopped me from trying to earn the approval of each person I remotely valued and, even if I didn't, I think I wanted everyone to like me because if they did, once again, it was reassurance that I was good. Do you see my two-year-old self making herself known?

I've come to understand that my trauma has enabled me to see the soul in everyone, acknowledging imperfections, yet looking beyond them to focus on their potential. This can be appropriate for some circumstances as long as I am also responding to the person as the human being they present themselves to be. I have worked to stop myself from trying to understand the people who were hurting me and to find

# UNDER THE ARMOR

meaning behind the pain they were projecting through their own suit of armor. I am no longer willing to put my own well-being on the back burner for people who are not willing to acknowledge the hurt their words and/or actions inflict on me.

How people treat you is a reflection of their own emotional maturity, self-awareness, past experiences, and current nervous system state. Hurt people, hurt people. Because we, as warriors, have gotten so used to anticipating the emotional state of others to ensure our own well-being, we tend to extend compassion and understanding, instead of setting boundaries and advocating for ourselves. We end up feeling resentful and angry, which we then struggle to process because we never really learned how to express those less than positive emotions. The cycle repeats, and the feelings continue to get buried under the layers of our armor. Eventually, the pressure builds and needs to be released, but since we refrained from expressing our needs to the people impacting us, we take it out on those we trust and love the most because there is a part of us that believes we won't lose them.

I spent so much time trying to avoid conflict with anyone outside my immediate family and to do my best to see the situation from a place of love and compassion, rather than resentment and contempt. Unless the other person was willing to express themselves from a mature place with a message coming from the heart, even if I might not agree, then I was likely to assume they didn't care and, in turn, I would be hurt. Whereas I feared losing control of my emotions and succumbing to tears in front of someone I was upset with, I noticed that I had no hesitation speaking my mind when I was triggered at home by one of my children.

What my son triggered in me was a reminder of all the men in my life who came before him who had never listened to me, made promises that they didn't keep, and, even if they said sorry, the one thing I could count on was that we would replay this scenario another time down the road. My release of anger toward my son was because he was "safe" for me. Even if he shut me out, he wasn't going anywhere. Recognizing this pattern allowed me to communicate with him, bridging the gap between control and trust. He is not my father, any of my exes, and, even though he reminds me of his father at times, he is and always will be his own person. It was never acceptable to dump on him the remnants of my unspoken needs, hurt, and anger that are associated with all the men who ever hurt me, and which I never had the courage or confidence to speak up to.

With my oldest daughter, our differing emotional expressions have become a learning curve. While I prefer immediate discussions, she leans towards privacy and silence. This dynamic, mirroring a previous passive-aggressive relationship with a mother-figure, raised questions about the wounds I might be creating for my children. I shared with my daughter how I feel when she shuts me out, but I also assured her that I respected her need for time to process her feelings. I want her to know that, although I don't always understand her, there is nothing wrong with her way of expressing herself. There are opportunities to understand one another in a mutual, respectful way. I would never want her to question herself, as I have spent much of my life doing.

Parents have conflicts with their children. Just like the partners we choose who reflect a variety of wounds, our children mirror the child inside us, and sometimes through our interactions we get a glimpse of our younger self trying to assert themselves in ways that they were prohibited from expressing in the past. The more we are aware of the triggers to our wounds and are able to identify and articulate our needs, the easier we will find shedding the armor in our relationships, allowing our connections with others to flourish, and those that no longer serve us can be pruned away to allow new growth.

# UNDER THE ARMOR

I once admitted to my children that I was aware of the harm I was inflicting. I had never done this parenting thing before, and I was still healing all the crap I carried with me from before I became a mother. I reminded them that it was they who chose me to be their guide in this lifetime and since I was acknowledging my failings, taking responsibility, and working on myself each and every day, I hoped that could count for something. It wasn't just for my children to hear that I knew how flawed I was, it was for me as well. Instead of shaming myself for being an inadequate mother, I chose grace, compassion, and forgiveness instead.

The difficulty lies in breaking old habits, not reverting to instinctual responses, and the ongoing struggle to pause before reacting. Instead of always trying to be strong and not let other people affect my mood, I can make choices about which battles are worth my time and energy. I can remain in the moment and not have one instance represent all past situations that I never addressed. I can actually identify what is upsetting me and allow myself to feel the emotions that had been stifled for so long, which enables me to be in the present circumstance, making it so much easier to sort through, address, and then release. The stakes are high – not just for me, but also for the well-being of my children. It's a constant effort to build relationships rooted in respect, appreciation, and love.

Today, I am able to say thank you to the human beings who have challenged me and reminded me of all the love I have surrounding me today. I thank these people for reminding me of how I stand in my values of integrity, kindness, and peace. I thank them for nudging me to journal, express myself, and to love myself more deeply rather than fixating on the flaws they had reminded me of. I am so grateful that I have grown so much over the years and have come to the place where I don't let other people knock me off course, begin to doubt myself, or make me feel like I am not worthy of being at the same table as anyone else.

I can see myself as a person who interacts with others openly, honestly, and vulnerably. I can look at the relationships I have cultivated with others and see that they are a reflection of what I have built over the years through my healing journey, and they are so beautiful. When I didn't love myself, I attracted some significantly toxic people and experiences. I did that. Now, the interactions I have with people, even quick encounters with strangers, are fulfilling, interesting, and positive. The world hasn't changed — I have.

Relationships can teach us so much about ourselves. They show us where our armor is most pronounced and not quite ready to be released. I want you to know that is absolutely okay. We didn't just wake up one day and put on a full suit of armor. It took time, and we have so many scars to show where we were vulnerable and were unprepared for the injuries we endured, some of them forced upon us and others, many others, unconsciously authorized by us to learn and heal from.

We all wear armor, and in relationships, these shields can become walls, muffling our calls for love and distorting our perception of others. As we shed this armor, expressing ourselves authentically, even when it's scary, allows for deeper connections. It's a journey, not a destination. There will be missteps, moments of retreat, and echoes of old wounds. But with each step forward, we chip away at the armor, revealing the beauty within.

This journey of self-discovery is a gift you can give yourself. Embrace your vulnerabilities, for they hold the key to deeper connections and a more fulfilling life. We all wear the marks of our experiences, and it's through these shared vulnerabilities that we find the strength to heal, connect, and truly thrive.

## UNDER THE
# ARMOR

## TRY THIS:
### Express Your True Feelings

In your next conversation with someone close to you, practice sharing your feelings openly and honestly. Notice if you start to put on emotional armor or hold back. Challenge yourself to express a genuine emotion or need, even if it feels vulnerable. This practice can help you build deeper, more authentic connections and slowly dismantle the barriers that keep you from fully engaging in your relationships.

Activity #6

# CANDICE KNIGHT

# PART 3

## THE WARRIOR WITHIN
Exploring the Experiences That Created Our Armor

# Chapter 7:
## Armor as a Buffer

*"People can only meet you as deeply as they have met themselves."*

## — Matt Kahn

In every relationship, two unique individuals carry their own armor, and that impacts perspectives and opinions.

If your upbringing, like mine, involved minimal control, the desire for control can become significant. Navigating this challenge involves mastering the art of effective communication for expressing your desires and needs, which can be difficult to convey clearly when muffled by our emotional armor. Equally important is recognizing those moments when silence is not just about listening, but also about understanding that **people can only meet you as far as they have met themselves.** This can be sorely disappointing when you are hoping to grow, heal, and move forward.

From a young age, my fixation on security was evident. Flipping through the pages of the Sears catalog, I delighted in selecting the essentials for my future home. From the furniture to the curtains, I noticed I had a practical taste. As an adult, I always ensured that I had more than enough toilet paper, canned goods, and that my bills were always paid on time and in full — a symbol of preparedness and responsibility, as well as a clear

# UNDER THE
# ARMOR

representation of my armor. I vividly recall the financial constraints as a child when, towards the end of the pay week, the more coveted treats like cookies and potato chips dwindled. My mom's cautionary reminders following each grocery haul echoed in my mind, urging my brother and me to make every last item stretch until the next payday. This lesson in stretching resources left a lasting imprint.

Following my mother's death, a substantial inheritance came my way. However, a lingering belief persisted—that once the money had been spent, I would be left to fend for myself, devoid of support. This reinforced my deeply rooted desire to stay prepared, a principle ingrained in me since childhood. It also kept me rooted in the limiting belief that money was finite and that if I didn't hold on tight to what I had, there would be no more coming in its place.

I've come to see how my choice of life partner reflected my wounds surrounding security. Self-awareness and understanding our motivations and resistance are key. Honest and vulnerable communication with partners can pave the way for healthy, fulfilling relationships that transcend past pain.

When I entered marriage, I hadn't yet committed to self-exploration, unaware that my wounds attracted a person revealing how I needed to heal. I was too busy crafting a seemingly successful life, my intentions stemming from fears rather than confidence and self-worth. Initial years of marriage were blissful, but eventually past relationship patterns resurfaced.

Our struggle lay in ineffective communication and conflicting views on security. The differences between our perceptions became apparent, which created a growing disconnect. In my vision, marriage meant forging a united front, a two-person team pursuing shared goals and dreams. Yet the challenge for me was reconciling the ideal I had in my mind with the reality of my actual life.

Forming a team became challenging when I believed that I had to shoulder everything independently, and when it seemed that everything was falling apart, the situation mirrored my own unraveling. Success in a relationship requires the collaboration of both individuals. While one person can seem to be the catalyst for the challenges, it's valuable to remind ourselves that, at one point, we had both believed we had found "the one." What many of us fail to take into consideration is that our happiness is our responsibility, as is our healing. **Until we are aware of our armor and do the work to explore what lies beneath it, we will unintentionally use it against our partner, creating a divide that many couples find impossible to bridge**.

Terms like gaslighting and narcissism often shift blame, diverting from deeper questions about why we chose certain partners in the first place. Relationship choices from behind armor often leave us with partners who evade responsibility and deflect blame, causing us to undermine our feelings. Many of us, in the guise of loyalty, remain in unhealthy relationships, not out of love or obligation, but as a reflection of our own unresolved wounds. Acknowledging this opens the gateway to profound self-discovery and healing.

When financial stress weighed on me, I'd bring it up with my partner, hoping to solve it together. Despite initial agreement, my hopes didn't materialize. Frustration led me to solve it solo, and I eventually stopped speaking up. These struggles—fear of scarcity, invalidated needs, inclination to shut down—manifested repeatedly. They were threads woven into my armor, appearing time and again.

No matter what I said, the security I sought wasn't coming from him. He seemed indifferent to my distress, so I took charge alone. This script was one I had written long before meeting him—a reality I

# UNDER THE ARMOR

convinced myself was the only one possible. My subconscious hope was for my partner to fill the security void left by my mother's passing. The challenge was that I wasn't aware of this underlying motivation, and my frustrations were fueled by a trauma begging to be acknowledged.

Later, I discovered he felt unappreciated and unheard, believing his efforts were never enough. The truth was a mix of his feelings and mine. Instead of labeling it as gaslighting, I see how my wounds magnified his pain. We both needed to look beyond blame, explore our feelings and needs, recognize the roots, and communicate effectively. It's not about who's right or wrong, but understanding each other's struggles and finding common ground.

To shield from pain, we hide behind our armor, attending to our needs without revealing vulnerability. Yet, this becomes absurd in relationships. While the intention is self-preservation, the truth is that, as humans, we have needs and a natural desire to communicate them to those who care about us.

We become accustomed to not being heard, suppressing feelings, projecting toughness, and soldiering on. Resentment builds, and we get defensive, feeling like no one cares. Sharing is crucial but must be done so people can truly receive. Not everyone can hold space for you. Break the cycle of insanity of repeating the same actions and expecting different results.

Trying to prove your worth or seeking understanding from someone who feels unheard is like speaking to a brick wall. The parts of you that are trying to be heard from beneath your armor need your attention because, until you fully understand it for yourself, no one else can give you what you need. **At the core, everyone yearns to be heard, to feel that their thoughts and words matter, but as long as you diminish, doubt, or question your value and worth, so, too, will other people.**

Sometimes, we believe speaking louder ensures understanding, or withdrawing prompts others to seek understanding. Unfortunately, this often leads us to function in ways that push people away, causing emotional pain to become a barrier in our relationships. When someone genuinely cares and offers support, it's challenging to believe it. On the other hand, if someone consistently shows an unwillingness or inability to listen and meet us halfway, there's an innate drive to keep trying, hoping they will eventually hear us. Through my journey, I realized that there were relationships I needed to let go of once and for all.

Something rarely discussed is that the peace that eventually surfaces when we begin to let go and release relationships comes at a cost. Shifting perspective from feeling like giving up to acknowledging the importance of emotional well-being over others' approval is crucial. Like a warrior, we don't leave comrades behind. The ultimate strength is choosing yourself and acknowledging the real battle lies within.

Choosing to face pain and grieve is an act of choosing oneself. It might be a journey through darkness, but genuine healing unfolds in our darkest moments. The value of this choice lies in the transformation from embracing our needs and well-being.

Every moment we spend tucking things behind our armor steals time from the life we desire. Allow everything to fall apart. Cease fighting for a life you've outgrown and trust that everything will be okay, even when the "how" or "when" remains unclear. Initially, things may feel messy and challenging. Embrace these feelings; they are part of the journey. The key is to go through it, embrace the process, and trust that removing the armor will pave the way for a brighter future.

Our emotional armor, while shielding, can hinder connection and growth. By understanding its roots and impact, we can choose a differ-

# UNDER THE
# ARMOR

ent path. Honest and vulnerable communication, along with self-compassion, are keys to building healthy, fulfilling relationships.

This journey isn't about blame, but taking responsibility for our happiness and healing. As we shed our armor and embrace vulnerability, we open ourselves to deeper connections, more effective communication, and genuine emotional intimacy. The path may be challenging, but the rewards—self-discovery, healthier relationships, and a life lived authentically—are worth the effort.

## TRY THIS:
Foster Vulnerable Communication

Identify a relationship where your emotional armor has impacted communication. Write down a few honest and vulnerable statements about your feelings or needs that you haven't expressed. Practice sharing these thoughts with the person involved, focusing on clear, compassionate communication. This practice can help dismantle emotional barriers and build deeper, more authentic connections.

Activity #7

# Chapter 8:
## How Our Armor Impacts Self-Care

*"The body keeps the score."*
### — Bessel van der Kolk

The armor we wear impacts how we care for ourselves.

To stay protected, we ignore messages from our body, mind, and soul, convincing everyone, including ourselves, that we are just fine. This facade of armored strength cloaks our darkened eyes and stooped shoulders, but underneath is a body that would collapse in relief if it felt safe to rest and be nurtured.

When I was in the hospital recovering from the car accident, my injuries required me to be bed bound for over a month. The armor removed for my physical healing was repurposed in order to shield my mind from having to process the tragedy, which is why I was able to entertain my friends and write my exams. As the days turned into weeks, I noticed that the soles of my feet began to crack and fall away. It was itchy and uncomfortable, yet intriguing at the same time. As each layer of unused skin began to fall away, what was revealed was the soft, tender surface, much like it must have been when I was a baby.

When the traction device was finally removed, a month and a half after I had first arrived, my legs wouldn't move. It was surreal to lose mobility

# UNDER THE ARMOR

and then struggle to regain it. As I learned to walk again, I began to once again harden the layers of my bare soles and built a new layer of armor to withstand life's challenges without my mother.

The memory of my mother's love kept me cushioned under the armor I wore and softened the blows of rejection I experienced as the years went by. After years of trying to convince others to love and care for me despite the fact that I remained hidden beneath my armor, I finally came to the realization that I didn't need to settle for scraps of love, but that in order to receive more I had to allow people to actually get to know me. Unfortunately, I don't think I really even knew myself.

Self-care is as basic as having a shower each day, but when you care for yourself with love, you take the time to soak in a bubble bath every now and then without feeling guilty for the time alone. As warriors we convince ourselves that there is no time to waste on getting our nails done, and that the money spent on a gym membership is frivolous when there are more practical expenses to take care of. Meanwhile, we encourage others to put themselves first even if we silently resent their ability to do so when we find little time for ourselves.

One day I had a vision of my body as a separate entity, listening to every word I uttered about it. Criticizing myself invoked a palpable heaviness and sadness, a silent plea for understanding. However, on the occasion I expressed love for myself, flaws and all, a spark ignited within, validating and appreciating the body that carried me through life. It became evident that seeking and waiting for external validation of our worth pales in comparison to the power of self-affirmation. **Until we appreciate ourselves, we will never really be able to accept the appreciation of others.**

Reflecting on how my statements might impact my body's well-being led me to a broader realization: I was consistently disregarding the signals my body tried to communicate. Whether it was the subtle cries for hydration, the nudges to get up and move, or the unmistakable signs urging me to prioritize self-care for restoration, I had consistently been overlooking these messages and concentrated my focus on the needs of others.

It can look like excess weight or a lack of sleep. It's pushing ourselves to the brink of exhaustion, yet we refuse to admit we need a break. In 2013, I realized that working out every day was my only strength. Just like when I was a youth, focusing on how to be successful in some way wasn't the worst way to cope, but it was so one-sided that all other areas of my wellness were languishing. Recognizing the importance of being my own number one priority changed everything, creating a ripple effect on those around me.

Giving myself permission to do what made me feel good without regret improved my well-being. As a teacher, the effort required to plan for a sick day often pushed me to show up to work rather than to stay home and get some rest. As a mother to young children, it was basically the same. The more I pushed through, the more resentful I became. My body would surrender during holidays, seizing the chance for rest.

Contracting Covid on Christmas day 2020 forced a ten-day quarantine from my kids, highlighting my need for self-care. Initially, I felt I should be productive. Being on my own was a perfect time to tackle those long overdue household duties. However, there was an unmistakable plea from my body, urging me to surrender to the couch, and indulge in Netflix. This plea resonated not just in my heart, but in the very physicality of my being, as my body seemed to struggle to stay alert or to engage in any movement at all.

My children's absence meant my sickness didn't compound into stress. The quiet of an empty home allowed me the space to focus on recovery, without the added strain of tending to their needs while unwell, which often turned into self-pity as I was caught in a battle between my armor reminding me of my duties and my body begging for comfort and care.

# UNDER THE ARMOR

This pattern had persisted over the years because it felt like ages since I had experienced genuine nurturing or care without strings attached, where I didn't feel like an imposition.

The story I had crafted was one of strength, independence, and an aversion to seeking help. Yet deep down, what I yearned for most was to be cocooned in a warm bed, with a comforting cup of tea and a tender kiss on my forehead. More than physical assistance, I craved the assurance that this moment of vulnerability wouldn't become ammunition against me in the future. I longed for the safety to embrace my fragile state without fear of judgment or exploitation.

Repressed emotions manifest physically or mentally, demanding our attention. Anxiety, stress, and depression often result from stifling emotions. Patterns emerge in life, and our bodies communicate answers if we listen. We must choose to stop repeating harmful behaviors and give ourselves permission to heal.

Allowing our armor to crack open reveals our true selves. We radiate differently when we genuinely love and care for ourselves. Relationships reflect our past and armor can prevent connection, but vulnerability allows authentic connections to be made most importantly to ourselves. Take a deep breath and begin.

# TRY THIS:
## Prioritize Genuine Self-Care

Reflect on recent self-care practices. Identify one small way to nurture your body, mind, or soul that you've been neglecting. Maybe it's taking a relaxing bath, spending time in nature, or reading a book for pleasure. Commit to this without guilt and observe how it makes you feel. Genuine self-care helps dismantle emotional armor and fosters a deeper connection with yourself.

Activity #8

# Chapter 9:
## Breaking Free from Limiting Beliefs

*"And the day came when the risk to remain tight in a bud was more painful than the risk it took to blossom."*

— **Anaïs Nin**

In 2004, my journey into teaching began, and in 2024, it ended. It is interesting that after one semester, I resigned for a more fitting opportunity: counseling at-risk students. Teaching wasn't my original calling; rather, it was the profound desire to be the supportive figure for teenagers that I yearned for when I was young—a caring adult who saw each student for who they were, not just based on the academic armor they wore.

The counselor role was perfect for me — until it became evident that it didn't support my desire for further growth and leadership. Armed with a master's degree and caring for a growing family, I faced a choice: continue with limited prospects or return to teaching for better pay. In 2009, I chose the latter, seizing every chance to escape the conventional classroom, eventually landing a position for teaching high school students through a local college. Securing this position brought tears of joy, believing it would transform my career and my life. Little did I know, the transformation would unfold in ways I hadn't anticipated.

Amidst my passion for ideas and collaboration, the reality of my role outside the community of teacher colleagues left me isolated, and virtually ignored. My armor served me well and allowed me to transform this isolation into a hidden blessing. The solitude afforded me precious downtime to delve into mindfulness techniques that led me to craft a course for my students and eventually birthed the concept of Phoenix Rising—a project that would eventually manifest into a business venture.

Despite my passion, I realized my supervisors didn't value my contributions. This prompted me to apply for a year-long sabbatical to explore my next steps apart from the confines of a system that failed to recognize my worth. Fate intervened when I became pregnant at 41, a miraculous 1 in 4,000 conception defying a ten-year-long vasectomy of my husband. Not only was my plan to take a year off to explore options for my future delayed, amidst the acceptance of impending motherhood, I learned that I would have to reapply for my position, an unexpected request since previously I had been told this position was mine for as long as I desired it. The outcome was as unforeseen as the pregnancy itself — I was not the selected candidate for the role. While the rejection hit hard, it turned out to be yet another hidden blessing.

Returning to the traditional classroom after my maternity leave, I balanced middle-aged motherhood with an undesired educational landscape. Despite attempts to find alternative roles, I realized it wasn't about my qualifications, but that my efforts were not valued. It took time, but finally the realization struck — it wasn't about them not wanting me, nor about me not being qualified enough. Just like other situations in which I attempted to prove my worth, my efforts would always fall short. They simply weren't interested in what I brought to the table. My grip on financial security began to ease, leading to a profound shift in perspective. I finally reached a pivotal moment where I acknowledged that my potential exceeded the confines of my current role.

In 2019, just as I was once again contemplating how to shift out of my career, my husband made a decision that added a profound layer of com-

# UNDER THE ARMOR

plexity to an already tumultuous time. Well aware of my dissatisfaction at work and my deep desire to expand my business, I thought we were united when we had discussions with a financial advisor to discuss next steps. It seemed as though we were a team as we strategized on managing our financial responsibilities, drawing from our past experiences while he pursued full-time education to become a registered nurse.

Fueling my enthusiasm, I had made plans to invest in a coaching program to expand my business beyond a hobby. I spent a weekend away learning more about this opportunity and mere hours after my return, following a heated conversation, he got in his car and drove away. At that moment, our marriage was over, and the dissolution of our union shattered the vision of partnership and support that I had held dear, casting me into an unexpected chapter of profound personal upheaval.

I had little time to get my armor back on and regroup, but instead of barreling back into the role I was so desperate to leave behind, I somehow ignored the reasoning to ask for a refund and put off my dreams yet again. The timeline to leave teaching was stretched once more, but amidst the uncertainty, I once again initiated preparations for a leave from employment. This phase marked a conscious choice to step into a future free from fear-driven security. Reflecting on my emotional armor, I realized the fear of financial instability stemmed from my mother's death and the financial security it had provided.

Growing up with financial struggles taught me frugality. My mother's passing brought an unexpected inheritance, allowing me to pursue education and independence. This fear of being alone motivated my drive for security. Shedding this armor revealed the pain I had ignored, pushing me to prioritize my dreams and security for my children.

Doubts about leaving my career extended beyond financial security to limiting beliefs about inadequacy, advanced age, and the haunting fear that, just as in my youth, no one would be there to help me if I needed it — all of this clouded my thoughts. Despite guilt and fear, I knew staying in the classroom was detrimental. I realized I had to break free from my career armor and embrace my purpose.

Letting go of my career uncovered wounds from my past. I realized I had honored my mother's legacy by ensuring my and my children's well-being. The doubts about leaving my career were entangled with limiting beliefs. I knew that remaining confined would be detrimental, so I embraced my potential beyond the classroom.

You may not need to leave your job, but your armor might hold you back within your career. If you end your day exhausted, you've lost yourself. Never forget to make time for what you love. A job is just a job, and you are replaceable. Getting under the armor associated with your ability to earn an income will reveal all the other skills and abilities you may have forgotten you have. As much as possible, leave work behind at the end of the day and embrace the life you want to create.

My journey through my education and career revealed my true potential. Armor is a sign of strength in navigating life's storms. Shedding layers revealed my passion and purpose beyond my comfort zone. Embrace the fullness of who you are to align with your purpose. Letting go of perceived security can uncover incredible opportunities.

This isn't just my story — it's a reminder that your story is still unfolding. Embrace the unknown with courage and belief in your worth. The world needs your unique talents, and you deserve to share them. Take a deep breath, step outside your comfort zone, and pursue your passions. The time is now.

# UNDER THE ARMOR

## TRY THIS:
### Challenge Your Limiting Beliefs

Identify a limiting belief that has held you back. Write it down, then write a counterstatement challenging this belief. Reflect on how this belief shaped your decisions and take one small step toward breaking free from it. This practice can help you unlock new opportunities and align more closely with your true potential.

Activity #9

# CANDICE KNIGHT

# THE ART OF SURRENDER
Initiating the Healing Process by Releasing Our Armor

# Chapter 10:
## Our Armor, Our Success

*"The oak fought the wind and was broken,
the willow bent when it must
and survived."*

### — Robert Jordan

Throughout my share of challenges and adversity, I was always aware of the strength within—the armor that allowed me not only to endure, but to thrive. As a child, I protected my mother against my father's drunken violence. During my hospital stay post-accident, I wrote my grade 10 exams, a testament to my determination even in the face of adversity. Despite encountering blatant racism in high school, I forged ahead, participating in the drama club, maintaining a job, and graduating as an Ontario scholar. Time and again, I demonstrated my ability to power through no matter what came at me.

My armor propelled me forward. With the sure step of the mountain goat, symbolic of the month I was born, I pursued knowledge relentlessly, earning multiple degrees. Even in moments of academic struggle, like the D I received in Statistics during my third year of university, I embraced the challenge, elevating it to an A. This perpetual drive, this "Type A, Get'er Done!" mentality, became both my shield and my sword.

Yet there came a time when the weight of perpetual accomplishment

# UNDER THE
# ARMOR

grew exhausting. Even a field of flowers will wither under the relentless heat of the sun. To continue pushing forward against resistance, driven by a need to conform, seeking approval, and reaching the top, eventually leads to burnout and dissatisfaction. I hit my own 'glass ceiling,' and the longer I tried to convince myself that one day I would feel fulfilled, the faster I burned out.

Deciding to leave my teaching career marked a departure from the known, and a hesitant step into the unknown. The panic of losing control crept in, challenging me to my core. I had spent my life striving for something tangible, and now there was a fog obscuring the steps ahead. It's a struggle between the comfort of purpose and the excitement of the unknown, a dichotomy we all grapple with at some point.

**The story of armor is one of resilience and grit, overcoming expectations, and achieving against the odds.** Initially, the goal was to prove my worth through education and professional success. The fear of relying on others pushed me to excel independently, a lesson I learned in my teen years.

The biggest challenge was shifting my mindset and releasing the belief that others' expectations mattered more than my own. As I took steps beyond the security I had created, the pressure intensified. My children became a tether to my sense of responsibility as a mother, which taunted my confidence in blazing a new trail. The financial burden of putting my son through university triggered deep-seated anxieties. Eventually, I realized that my children are on their own personal paths, and I don't have to carry the weight of their journey alone.

The obstacle wasn't just financial — it was a battle for independence and dignity. I continued to feel bound by societal expectations that had begun with equating success with university education and later earning a professional designation. The fear of being viewed as selfish or crazy for leaving a secure, high-paying career with benefits and a pension weighed heavily. Overcoming this required acknowledging that my potential growth was limited in my existing space.

Letting go is the catalyst for the next phase of success. Dreaming big, releasing control, and saying 'Yes!' to the path ahead is transformative. If it were easy, we'd all enjoy the possibilities afforded by taking a chance on ourselves and believing in positive outcomes. Can you imagine?

From a higher perspective, I see how unbelievable my life has been despite the interference of my armor. In fact, it allowed me to achieve great things, and I am grateful. However, where I am meant to go next doesn't require proof of capability. I don't need to strive or try, I just need to be and to say 'Yes!' when my heart lights up, and trust that when my armor invites doubt into my mind, I can trust that I am the right person for the task at hand. I was born for this, and I no longer need armor to believe I am prepared. Being open, vulnerable, and trusting is the key.

We are enough. We always have been. The reason it seemed otherwise is that we didn't believe it, so neither did anyone else. Even if they did, we didn't trust them. From now on, the only person you don't want to let down is yourself. Moving forward with integrity and love, even when making mistakes, is absolutely okay. The person you want to make proud is yourself. **You are all the approval and validation you need.** Praise from others is nice, and you'll receive it with gratitude, knowing you did a great job even if no one noticed. You are doing exactly what you came here to do. Shedding your armor brings you the clarity and confidence to do that.

At some point, we realize we have done all we can in a certain area of life. It becomes stifling, and to reach the next level of success, we must let go of what no longer serves us. Releasing another layer of armor is necessary. While it takes time, dedication, and commitment to get where we want to be, this time the focus is on something long neglected—ourselves.

# UNDER THE
# ARMOR

Armor may get us through tough times, but eventually, it can become a cage. Your story is a testament to both the power and limitations of resilience. Releasing the need for constant achievement opens the door to a different kind of success—one built on self-compassion, authenticity, and living in alignment with your true purpose. The door is open, you simply need to cross the threshold.

This journey of shedding armor isn't about discarding strength. It's about evolving it. You've proven your capability; now trust your intuition and embrace the vulnerability that fuels genuine connection and growth. The greatest validation comes from within. By honoring your own needs and desires, you pave the way for a future filled with purpose, passion, and the exhilarating freedom of being truly you.

# TRY THIS:
## Recognize When to Shed Your Armor

Reflect on a time when your resilience and determination helped you overcome a challenge. Acknowledge the strength your armor provided, but also consider if holding onto it is still serving you. Identify one area in your life where letting go of this protective layer could open up new opportunities for growth and connection. Taking small steps towards vulnerability can lead to greater self-compassion and authenticity.

Activity #10

# Chapter 11:
## Armor as a Stepping Stone

*"Letting go isn't getting rid of.
It's making room for something better."*

**— Unknown**

I like to imagine that the universe tries to communicate with us all the time, but most people are unaware. It begins with a whisper—a fleeting thought we often ignore. Then, the message becomes a gentle nudge, but still, we shrug it off. It's probably nothing.

In our daily hustle, we wear invisible armor, shielding us from the subtle messages the universe sends, dismissing them as coincidences. But what if, by peeling away our armor, we could become more attuned to these whispers, allowing the universe's guidance to shape our journey? If we fail to listen, the universe steps up the game, giving us a harder slap to wake us up. Hopefully, we take notice and follow the divine calling.

Whether we do or don't, we often return to old habits and patterns, leaving the universe no other choice but to run us over with a Mack truck. If you haven't gotten to the Mack truck moment yet, or you made it out a little worse for wear, you now have a chance to get yourself together and choose to tune in rather than tune out.

Back in 2013, my relationship with my family was crumbling, and my marriage was falling apart. It had been years in the making, but at the time, my family issues made me need my husband more. Balancing his career, education, partnership, and fatherhood created insurmountable stress. These events exacerbated existing cracks, turning them into gaping chasms we couldn't bridge. Despite the turmoil, it must have been only a slap from the universe. The Mack truck of my marriage hadn't struck yet.

I won't go into details because everyone has their own story. What matters is our perception and the meaning we give it. For years, I felt estranged from my family, holding on through ups and downs until I was ultimately rejected. The devastation was extreme. I used to say this loss was worse than losing my mother because the people I loved chose to exclude me. It took another six years before I finally let go, realizing I would no longer settle for a text message on my birthday, when I wasn't welcome to visit. Letting go prepared me for my husband leaving for our third and final separation. It's like a layer of armor comes off, only to be put back on, until we realize nothing will change until we do.

There is a story I once heard about a man who visits his neighbor's house and notices the man's dog whining as if hurt. He asks what is wrong with the dog. His neighbor replies that the dog is sitting on a nail. Surprised, the man asks why the dog doesn't get off the nail, and the neighbor shrugs, saying, "I guess it doesn't hurt enough."

If you have been hurting for longer than you can remember, isn't it time to say 'Enough!', get off the nail, and take care of the wounds it inflicted? **Our armor helps us withstand pain and negativity, but deep down we all crave peace, calm, and love for who we are.** We can't have these things unless we get under the armor and expose our true selves.

Navigating self-discovery often leads to realizing that some connections must be released as we heal and grow. Acknowledging that parting ways is in our best interest doesn't diminish the emotional weight it carries. As

# UNDER THE
# ARMOR

we evolve, recognizing and honoring the grief accompanying farewells becomes crucial to leveling up. Each departure is a testament to profound changes within us, reminding us that growth involves letting go of external ties and the emotions tethered to them. It is in grieving these losses that we affirm every release as a step towards our authentic rebirth.

My journey exposed how often we miss the universe's whispers. Invisible armor shields us from its nudges, dismissed as coincidences. But the universe persists, urging us to wake up. Like my 2013 wake-up call with family and marriage, sometimes it takes a "slap" to get our attention.

We tend to cling to connections that hurt, like the dog on a nail. The discomfort becomes unbearable because deep down, we all crave peace, harmony, and acceptance. Shedding our armor, like letting go of unhealthy relationships, allows our true selves to emerge and attract connections that support our growth.

Growth often involves letting go because, as we evolve, some connections no longer resonate. Grieving these farewells is crucial. Each departure reflects our inner transformation, a reminder that growth involves releasing what we have outgrown. By embracing the emotions that arise, we affirm each layer shed as a step towards our authentic selves.

# CANDICE KNIGHT

## TRY THIS:
Tune into Subtle Messages

Take a moment each day to sit quietly and listen to your inner thoughts. Reflect on any recurring ideas or feelings you might be dismissing as coincidences. These subtle messages might be guiding you towards important realizations or changes in your life. Pay attention and consider how these whispers could be urging you to shed your armor and embrace personal growth.

Activity #11

# Chapter 12:
## The Scars of Our Survival

*"Scars have the strange power to remind us that our past is real."*

## — Cormac McCarthy

I don't recall exactly when I started consciously paying attention to my thoughts about myself. Over the years, the words and actions I directed toward myself were often unkind. As layers of armor chipped away, it eventually became natural for me to look in the mirror, at every part of myself, and declare out loud that I loved and accepted all that stood before me.

This was a transformative act, a shedding of the invisible armor I had unknowingly worn against my own being. I apologized to myself for all the times I had been cruel and unkind, recognizing that the armor was not a shield, but a barrier to self-love. I also told as many parts of myself as possible why I appreciated them, stripping away the layers that had concealed my genuine appreciation for the unique aspects that make me whole.

The first imperfection I noticed was something I was born with. When my mom was pregnant with me, people joked she would have a zebra baby because she was White and my father was Black. I came out with a birthmark covering a large portion of skin on the left side of my upper body. It isn't shocking, but it is noticeable. I wonder what my parents thought when they saw me for the first time.

My youngest child, Lucy, was born with a perfect circle birthmark on her cheek and a small, straight line across her belly. I told her the mark on her face, now faded, was a kiss from an angel who loved her very much.

I have three scars on the side of my nose from chicken pox. I had been warned not to scratch them, but like most kids I did and now I have proof of enduring that pesky childhood affliction. I have a few other scars from childhood injuries. As an 80's kid, I am lucky to have survived at all—no helmets! There are also stretch marks from growing fast during puberty, gaining weight, and being pregnant.

I have big scars on my right leg, which was shattered in the car accident. They remind me I survived, and I am grateful to my body for recovering physically so I can walk. I am not very good at crossing my legs, but I can walk, and after being in traction for more than a month and having to learn to walk again, I can tell you that I'll take what I have and never complain.

I have a scar above my pubic bone from birthing all three of my children. I longed for a natural home birth, but my kids were born perfect and healthy through c-sections. I healed, and it is part of who I am. It isn't just the scar that has been reopened three times — it is the soft flap of skin above the tightened scar tissue that made me consider a "mommy makeover" briefly. Instead, I chose to accept it along with all the other bodily changes I've noticed as I age.

I have scars on my face, back, and other areas from acne and picking at sores. This is me being vulnerable. I once read an article about skin picking, and my heart broke. The person described was me—a perfectionist coping with stress. I wish these scars would go away, and though they have faded, the pigmentation difference reminds me of the woman who did her best to make it through the day. I no longer feel the need to cover up with makeup. I am not ashamed. Acne and other inflammatory conditions are tied to

# UNDER THE
# ARMOR

holding back emotions that need release, such as anger and worry. Toxicity needs to go somewhere — if not let out, it finds a way.

Finally, there are scars I can't show you. I am trying to be more willing to let them be seen, but it's still challenging. These are the scars of my heart. They run deeper and are still healing. I am exposing many through this book, but some can only be shared with those who love me most. There are some that will always be only for me to see. You have those, too, I'm sure.

Bear your scars proudly, as badges of strength. They are imprints of battles won and lessons learned. Your armor has weathered storms, but it is not a fortress to hide behind—it's a testament to your resilience. **Your scars, visible and unseen, tell stories of survival and growth.** Never feel the need to explain them to anyone, for they are part of your unique journey. However, profound healing occurs when you allow others to witness and understand your scars. Just as armor shields, it can also become a bridge connecting hearts. Trust in the power of vulnerability. In sharing your battles, you may find solace and a collective strength that mends wounds better and faster than solitude ever could.

We all wear armor, sometimes directing it at ourselves. Imperfections can become a record of our journey. Stretch marks, scars, and birthmarks—each tells a story of resilience. Even the hidden scars of the heart, though deeply personal, are testaments to the battles we've fought.

Vulnerability, though challenging, holds the power to connect us. Sharing our battles, even the unseen ones, allows others to witness our collective resilience and builds bridges of understanding. Solace and healing can be found not just in self-acceptance, but also in knowing we are not alone through our sharing.

## TRY THIS:
### Embrace Your Scars

Stand in front of a mirror and acknowledge your physical and emotional scars. Reflect on the stories they tell and the strength they represent. Write down one positive affirmation about each scar, embracing them as symbols of resilience and growth. Consider sharing one of these stories with someone you trust, fostering deeper connection and mutual understanding.

Activity #12

# Chapter 13:
## Stifled by Our Armor

---

*"You are not your past.*
*You are more than that.*
*You are who you choose to be."*

**— Moana**

Obstructed by our armor, our emotions struggle to find their true voice, creating a barrier that muffles our feelings and prevents open, effective communication. Much like a fog that clouds a mirror, these protective layers unintentionally obscure the genuine expression of our needs and feelings. Being aware of this impact is essential if we want to express ourselves honestly and receive a response unblocked by our defenses.

Despite the work I have done to remove layers of my emotional armor, I'm still learning how to express anger and process it in a healthy way. Most people might say the same. As children, we expressed any emotion we felt at any given moment. For me, anger was the one that wasn't really allowed. I felt it, but I didn't feel safe expressing it. I'm not exactly sure when that became my truth, but I'll attribute it to the haphazard construction of protection by my 2-year-old self.

A memory that comes to mind is my dad expressing his anger toward my mom. My dad likely held his frustrations in and used alcohol, other substances, and work to numb whatever he was feeling. Instead of processing his emotions, these methods gave him an excuse to let everything out all at once toward my mother, the person he felt safest with, but who probably triggered him the most.

I witnessed many of my father's angry outbursts, and they were scary. As a young child, I thought he appeared like Te Fiti did to Moana in the Disney movie—a vicious, unapproachable monster. He was physically and verbally abusive to my mom. Though the details have thankfully faded, the memories remain, lurking beneath my armor and impacting how I process my own fiery feelings. While anger can initiate change, how it is expressed affects what happens next. To me, underneath anger is hurt and betrayal. Anger arises when you feel unseen, unheard, undervalued, or disrespected. We all want to be acknowledged in a way that makes us feel that we matter.

My expression and processing of anger requires more of my love and attention. I noticed that one way I dealt with my anger was by projecting my feelings onto myself, my partner, and my children. Sadly, the way I expressed my feelings often didn't match what I was actually upset about. I was reactive and took my rage out on the people I loved most because I felt safe enough to let it all out with them. **It's difficult to admit, but I can see it, feel it, and continue to heal it**. I recognize how far I have come and actively improve how I communicate my feelings with the people in my life.

Maybe you, too, are a projector. You might project your anger onto someone, put it into an activity, or take it out on yourself. I have projected my frustrations onto my family before. I'm sure there were times I resembled Te Fiti myself. Nearing the end of my last semester as a teacher, I took my irritation home, snapping at my kids more than usual. It wasn't good, so I did a few things to alleviate the stress and not bring it home with me.

Under our emotions lies a need. Maybe, like me, your needs were dismissed, shamed, or ridiculed, which is why your anger might take over and become more than you ever expected, hurting others in its wake. It's

# UNDER THE
# ARMOR

up to you to stop, breathe, and maybe step away. It's okay to be angry and hurt, but what is the actual source of that emotion? Are you mad at what you think, or do you need to dig deeper? Te Fiti needed something from Moana that had been taken from her, making her into a monster, but it's up to us to find what needs to be healed within ourselves.

When we shove our anger and hurt behind our armor, it becomes trapped, stifled, and builds up over time. Despite what we may have been led to believe, anger is not a bad thing. Think about how you process anger. Do you try to avoid it altogether? It comes up, you notice it, but you don't want to make things worse, so you tell yourself it's not a big deal and you should just get over it. Maybe you do the opposite and hold onto it like a precious keepsake, reminding yourself of all the wrongs you have endured. Or maybe you are triggered by the smallest infraction yet your response explodes like a volcano. Instead of healing, ignoring the true source of this anger keeps it flourishing, rather than taming it and revealing the pain it is protecting.

You must take responsibility for how your challenging emotions are processed and how they might impact others. That can be difficult, and you must be careful not to get caught in a pit of blame and self-reproach. Bring your attention back to your body. If it's already spilled out and gotten out of hand, then as soon as you catch yourself, stop. Just stop. You don't have to keep going. Take a moment, a time out, and then say what you need to say.

Your feelings matter, all of them. They are there to show you what works for you and what doesn't. They are your best guide because they come before you even think about things. The more willing you are to deconstruct that armor from a patient, understanding, and loving space, the more you give yourself permission to figure yourself out. Nothing looks the same once it has been broken down to its basic components. Making the effort to analyze and interpret this aspect of our armor reveals a different perspective.

It's tough, I know, but please keep going. You are worth it. It's time for you to remind yourself of that. When you change how you look at your darker side, you'll see it isn't so bad, dark, and dangerous. These aspects of you will reveal themselves as the pain you have been afraid to acknowledge. But if you want to heal, the validation of your truth needs to come from you.

## TRY THIS:
Process Your Emotions Mindfully

The next time you feel a strong emotion, such as anger or frustration, take a moment to pause and breathe deeply. Instead of reacting immediately, try to identify the underlying need or wound this emotion is highlighting. Write down your thoughts and feelings to gain clarity. This practice can help you understand and express your emotions more constructively, leading to healthier interactions and deeper self-awareness.

Activity #13

# Chapter 14:
## Integrating All Aspects of Self

*"What you can't be with, won't let you be."*
## — Debbie Ford

Imagine our shadow side as the obscured underbelly of our armor, representing the concealed aspects of ourselves that often evade the light of conscious awareness. It holds the unexplored recesses of our psyche, securing suppressed emotions, unresolved traumas, and hidden fears. Just as the shadow of an object is cast where light cannot reach, our shadow side thrives in the unilluminated corners of our consciousness. It beckons for acknowledgment, urging us to delve into the depths of self-discovery and confront the concealed elements that influence our thoughts and actions.

I remember asking someone if they had at least one friend they could be "ugly" with. To me, that meant a person you could trust to see the full uncensored version of yourself—the emotional, negative, desperate, unhinged you. I thought it made complete sense until someone challenged me.

While in Estonia, I participated in a workshop exploring the different aspects of ourselves. The facilitator referred to them as our positive and negative sides, which I ended up changing to our soul and shadow sides. We made a chart, and at the top we put the highest reflection of ourselves. To the right and left were various aspects that presented themselves based on circumstance or need. The other side of the chart represented those darker aspects of ourselves that we were less likely to put front and center for others to see, or even for ourselves to acknowledge.

At the end of it all, I shared a bit of what had come up for me and casually referred to my shadow aspects as that "ugly" part of me. There was the lone child who felt she didn't fit in and wasn't good enough. There was her victim side, which had convinced her she had to be a martyr and sacrifice her needs and wants for everyone else. There was the wounded part, the passive-aggressive part, the aggressive part, and there was a side of me that was numb. That part was me all tucked behind my armor, desensitized to the difficulties ahead because I had come to expect life to be hard and that I would face all challenges on my own. Yeah…that was me. Sigh.

What the workshop facilitator heard was a woman who subconsciously downplayed her struggles and was unable to see the strength and resilience, maybe even the beauty, in her shadow side. She asked if I had ever considered the 14-year-old me who had lost her family in a car accident and had to recover from her own major injuries. What about the 17-year-old me who was told to get out of her family's home because supporting a traumatized teen was more than they could continue to provide? There was the me who had been cheated on more than once and was left alone just when she was hoping to jump into a career change, assuming she would be supported by her partner. I told her to stop. She took a deep breath and said she wished I could see what she saw.

I hated every moment of this armor stripping. I never consented to this. I didn't know her, and she sure as hell didn't know me. I wanted to escape, so I thanked her, gave a little chuckle, and packed up my things. Then she had the nerve to ask if she could give me a hug. The nerve. Who did she think she was? When I was safe back in my Airbnb, I cried. I was mortified that a stranger had been able to see me so clearly and had more compassion for these parts of myself that I had just referred to as ugly. I guess my

# UNDER THE
# ARMOR

soul decided I was ready, and it wasn't the last time this would happen while I was at this conference.

I tell you all this because maybe you have had this feeling of being unexpectedly exposed. I'm really good at "seeing" other people, but I'm also really good at hiding myself. I allow myself to be just vulnerable enough that people are satisfied and don't ask any questions or feel the need to add their thoughts about me to the conversation. I seem to have a way of sharing something personal and then turning the focus to the other person. I have been told that was how I created a safe space for people to be vulnerable. I suppose that going to a three-week self-development conference was meant to get me out of my comfort zone in more ways than one.

This was just the beginning, and even though I had begun to acknowledge my shadow part as something other than just ugly, I still resisted embracing and integrating it as part of my highest self. A year later, I became acquainted with my beautiful shadow self when a person I sought guidance from drew a diagram to illustrate how my anger was outside my core self. She said that by keeping it at bay, I was reducing my self-confidence and ability to set boundaries. There was someone in particular she emphasized that I needed to be more assertive with.

I responded with confusion because, in my mind, I had fully accepted my shadow self and had been creating clearer boundaries than ever before. I had forgotten that just a month prior, while in Guatemala, a shaman doing a sacred Mayan reading for me informed me that the abuelos had given him a message that there was still a debt not yet filled with a past partner. As long as that stood unresolved, I would not be able to move on. I just couldn't see what more I could do to prove that I was healed, had moved on, and was ready to get on with my life.

Finally, just after Christmas, I think I finally got the message. My astrologer had come by to go over my astrocartography chart, but before he got started, I shared with him something that had come up with my ex a couple of hours earlier. He got a dead serious look on his face and told me I would not be able to move on unless I stood in my power once and for all and stopped trying to make everything "nice," even when treated with disrespect. I was pissed! I thought I had done everything I needed to do, yet here was the message again, more blatant than ever before.

I was still avoiding potential conflict with someone I knew would not have a civil conversation with me. I tried to make things easy for the sake of my kids and yet had been told by my oldest to stop being nice all the time. Nothing was changing, and if nothing changed, maybe I was still not ready to move beyond this karmic lesson. I wasn't just pissed—I was devastated!

My astrologer friend went on to say that I continually put myself in a submissive role to make peace. As soon as he said that, I was reminded of my inner puppy dog rolling over on her back as a symbol of compliance and obedience. I had been giving away my power and silencing my truth. I thought it had been to create peace for the sake of my children, but the chaos I was creating for myself was impacting my children. My desire to make the discomfort disappear by dealing with disrespect enabled it to continue.

I needed this wake-up call. I imagine my higher self just above me beyond the veil of reality, patiently guiding me along the way. I picture her rooting for me, supporting me, and comforting me as needed. When I imagine her response to my resistance to embracing my power and standing firm in my limits, I see her shaking her head in bewilderment when I become a child-like version of myself, making myself small and easy to take advantage of. I keep repeating the same pattern by silencing my anger, and instead of saying no, I say, "What can I do so that you won't be such a jerk to me?"

I am not a victim, nor am I unwilling to change, but I am trying to un-

# UNDER THE
# ARMOR

learn a lifetime of traumatic responses and avoid the pain that comes with standing in my truth. As we stop cowering beneath our armor we must begin to embrace our shadow, seeing how far we still have to go before we fully understand how brilliant we are. Our brilliance can even be found in the shadow, because it is that part of us that steps in front of our light so it is not shared with those who will not appreciate it. If you don't look at all aspects of yourself and embrace them as essential to your character, you will remain fragmented. The more fragmented, the less connected you feel to your higher self, interrupting the flow of your journey forward. Aren't you ready to be on track?

We all think we have done so much to mend our wounds and heal our hearts, but if you're reading this book, you are just now ready to do the real work. You need to not only see your shadow side, but embrace it and invite it in as a valued part of yourself. Your armor has given those parts of you even more darkness to lurk behind. Bring all of it into the light. When you are outside in the sunshine, your profile creates a shadow. We used to delight in that when we were young. When it pops up, it needs to be seen by you with love, acceptance, forgiveness, and most definitely some gratitude.

## TRY THIS:
Embrace Your Shadow Self

Take a moment to reflect on the aspects of yourself you typically hide or deny. Write down these "shadow" traits and consider how they have protected or served you in the past. Next, practice self-compassion by acknowledging these parts of yourself with love and acceptance. This exercise can help you integrate your shadow, fostering greater self-understanding and emotional resilience.

Activity #14

# Chapter 15:
## Finding Freedom in Vulnerability

*"The only way to win at life is to
let down the walls, embrace the vulnerability, and
love the people who can handle the truth of you."*

— C. JoyBell C.

Our armor is like a skilled storyteller, spinning intricate tales that we convince ourselves to be true so that we can share them with the world. It creates illusions, shielding us from vulnerability, and presenting a well-crafted version of ourselves. This deceptive facade distorts our perception of reality and conceals our raw authenticity beneath its protective layers. Telling someone we're fine when we absolutely aren't, or saying yes instead of no, are examples of using our shield to speak for us rather than being honest. Think of all the little white lies told to avoid hurting someone's feelings or making us look "bad." These are just more layers of protection that keep us from being fully in our power.

We often say and do things that aren't truly representative of what we need, want, or feel at the time. We do this because we think we need to show that we care about someone and spare them from feeling burdened by us. We want to be useful, helpful, and understanding, and we sure as heck don't want to look bad or be a bother. Over time, this makes us resentful, and it's our own damn fault because we aren't willing to deal with the possibility that someone may not like what we have to say. Worse yet, they may decide they don't like us.

This has shown up in so many ways and with so many people, and I am still awaiting the time when putting down my shield during conflict will matter the most, which is when I am in a romantic partnership. In the meantime, I can continue to practice with all the other people who care about me. It is one thing to respond to a stranger's inquiry into our well-being with a "fine, thank you," but when it comes to people who are actually invested in us, it begins to build a wall of defense that becomes impenetrable.

I became so accustomed to downplaying or dismissing my feelings as irrelevant or unimportant, but they would seethe inside me just waiting to be released. I can see how I did this every time I pushed myself when unwell, then displaced my frustrations on my children because I felt an external expectation, even though it was only coming from within. It was evident when I would stress about how the expenses would be covered because I felt that the financial responsibility fell solely on me. It was in the explanation I made when I changed my mind about going out because, even though I wanted nothing more than to be curled up in my bed, I was afraid to let my friend down because my armor had convinced me they would never understand.

The crazy thing is I don't think that people caught up in our pretenses are even really aware. I mean, seriously, not everyone is intuitive and able to read minds. Okay, most people aren't even empathetic enough to sense that someone is in need, or maybe it's just so much easier to take people at face value because that keeps things from getting messy, and who wants to get involved in someone else's feelings, anyway?

I held back so much pain as a teen, doing all the things I thought would make it look as if I was okay. I had a job, was involved in the drama club, got good grades, and had "friends" (I put that in quotations because I was

# UNDER THE ARMOR

just trying to get by). I stayed in my room a lot, listening to music, writing out my feelings, and convincing myself that my mother wouldn't want me to end my life even if it seemed that everyone else would be better off without me. What I wanted was to have someone to talk to, to feel safe with, and to be able to share vulnerably.

I tried so hard to be small and quiet, but that's not me, so it always felt like I was pissing people off. I actually had the courage to write a letter trying to express myself to my family members, but when I was asked to have a conversation about it with them, I was not met with love and concern. I walked away feeling worse than before. I felt so unloved and unwanted. That part of me is still grieving and healing, but, luckily, I love that teenager so much I think she feels it deep inside me.

My deepest wounds told me I was unwanted and easy to get rid of. I came to believe that no one would ever fight for me, which is why I put my armor on to begin with. The point of getting under the armor is to stop hiding behind it because you are worried what others will think. Eventually, you will hopefully accept that it is better to just let things be, let people go, and stop fighting for explanations and apologies. **You'll begin to stand in your truth rather than adjusting it to meet the needs of others**.

I had to take baby steps, and part of that meant just saying no when I felt it. I also learned to check in with myself as to why I was choosing to decline. Was it because the task was something I truly wasn't interested in, or was it my armor trying to keep me in line with my comfort zone? It was so empowering to say no to extra volunteer duties at work which, in the past, I would have committed to. I had wanted to be seen as a team player, a go-getter, and an employee who treated her role as more than just a job. Those days had left me drained and feeling unappreciated, so when I did extras, it was because I truly wanted to. **People will take as much as you give, so it's up to you to make your limits clear.**

Stop chasing people or wasting time trying to get them to understand, because the odds are that the people you are spending all this time and energy on are going to do exactly what you expect them to do—disappoint you. Sometimes you have to accept the apology that you will never get. Even if you are certain of how things played out, everyone else has their perspective, even if it makes no sense to you. What I do know is my truth is mine, and what I want you to do more of is to honor yours.

The freedom of releasing yourself from the armor is that you start to have more people around you who actually want to get messy with you. They will ask questions and come in for those awkward hugs. If they aren't the touchy-feely type, they will find another way to show you how much they care about you and how much you matter to them. As you become more accepting and loving of yourself, guess what? You will be more comfortable accepting affection from others, and you will end the pretenses and say what you really feel, exactly in the way you need to say it.

Begin by nurturing an authentic connection with yourself! Shed the people-pleasing tendencies and embrace the courage to release what no longer serves your needs or aligns with the evolving person you are becoming. Just like a garden can't thrive when overrun by weeds consuming nutrients and sunshine, our lives can't flourish when burdened with layers of armor fortified on the expectations we have created in our minds.

Looking back, my teenage self desperately craved a safe space for vulnerability. Someone to see beyond the armor, the good grades, and the forced smiles. That's the beauty of shedding these layers—it allows for genuine connection. It won't always be easy. There may be misunderstandings, awkward hugs, and moments where honesty stings. But beneath that discomfort lies a profound freedom, the freedom to be fully seen, loved, and accepted for who you truly are.

This journey of vulnerability may start small—a simple "no" or a heart-

# UNDER THE
# ARMOR

felt conversation. But with each step, you'll cultivate more authentic connections. People who see your worth, not a carefully constructed persona. People willing to get messy, share their truths, and build a foundation of trust. Remember, your truth is powerful. Honoring it allows others to honor theirs. So shed the armor, embrace your vulnerabilities, and step into a life filled with genuine connection and self-acceptance. It's a journey worth taking.

## TRY THIS:
Practice Vulnerable Communication

In your next meaningful conversation, be honest about your feelings and needs. Instead of hiding behind a facade or telling a little white lie, express yourself openly and genuinely. Notice the response and how it feels to share your truth. This practice will help you build deeper connections and gradually dismantle the armor that keeps you from being fully yourself.

Activity #15

# Chapter 16:
## The Battle Between Armor and Authenticity

*"Let everything happen to you: beauty and terror.
Just keep going. No feeling is final."*

**— Rainer Maria Rilke**

You may have been consciously exploring and dismantling your armor for a while now. Let me assure you, this process is undeniably worthwhile. It's important to also acknowledge that it isn't an effortless path, and there may be numerous layers still awaiting discovery.

Your commitment to this process reflects your dedication to personal growth. At times, you might sense resistance or find yourself retreating; it's like you have both armor and a sword, prepared for a battle—a battle that, nowadays, you realize is most often internal.

Trust in your journey, even in moments when it feels like you're retracing your steps.

I have to tell you with all honesty that this armor removal is not a linear process, from point A to point B. It is a continuous journey of self-exploration filled with moments of uncertainty, challenges, and setbacks.

Your motivation diminishes from time to time, and when you feel that you are in a great place, something comes up to remind you that this 'life

# UNDER THE ARMOR

thing' is filled with ebbs and flows. Those ebbs can knock your stability out from under you, and those flows can have you second-guessing that things can really be this good. These challenges are opportunities for deeper healing, greater self-awareness, and a boost of self-love.

It feels odd to be writing a book about getting under our protective armor and realizing that I have done enough of that at least for now.

I'm finally ready to take what I've learned into the next adventure, which is not just a turn of a page in the chapter of my life. This book is a literal representation of my life. These stories need to be shared and released because I am ready to move on. Where I've gotten to in my journey — by allowing the hero within to be freed — has prepared me for the passage to the next level of my life.

I have shared with you so many different aspects of what I have learned over the years — and I want to continue being honest, especially because where I am now is the greatest test of what I have learned. I have been psyching myself up to taking this leap of faith for a while now, and recently things have gotten real. Three years ago, I began preparing for a year-long paid leave of absence, which I am now in the midst of.

At first, I thought I would go back for a final year, since my contract stipulates that you are expected to return to work for at least as long as you were away. Over the last three years — and what brought me to this desire to leave my career — it has never been clearer that it is not in my best interest to return.

More than a year ago, I met a gentleman who runs a writer's retreat in Guatemala, and I promised myself that I would go. I always knew I would write a book, and this seemed the perfect opportunity to have all aspects of the process covered, even up to the publication of my finished product. Here I am, for a whole month, waking up every morning with the view of a lake and volcanoes all around.

Why then am I filled with dread at different points during many of my days?

At some point each day, it pops into my mind that I have no clue what is happening next, and it scares me a lot. Each day, when this happens, I remind myself to be in the moment. I recall all the amazing things that just seem to randomly pop up and guide me into the next step on my path.

As I looked back on the challenges I faced on my life journey, it still seemed as though things would just find a way of working out. I would tell people that no matter what I was dealing with — and man, I had a lot going on! — it still seemed as though I was skipping down the yellow brick road.

What IS the yellow brick road?

Sure, it's what Dorothy went down in The Wizard of Oz or The Wiz (the Motown version), but what did Dorothy find at the end?

I never thought about this aspect until recently, long after I used this metaphor to describe my life. Dorothy, on her perilous journey, found her strength, her courage, and her own inner wisdom, and by the end of it all, she had found herself. Before she made her way back to Kansas, she had to face the greatest challenge of all.

She stood up to the Wizard for herself and her friends, and then she risked losing it all for her dog, Toto, only to find out in the end that she had the magic with her all along to get where she longed to be.

Right now, my higher self — the universe, or even my own personal Wizard of Oz — is calling me to stop hiding behind my armor and to embrace the unknown with confidence and the certainty that I will be exactly

# UNDER THE ARMOR

where I am meant to be. This armor that I've been telling you about, along with the battle between my hopes and fears, has me on edge and gets me caught up in my head. So, each day I take a breath, talk or write it out, and get back to the moment I am currently in.

When you are in the thick of it — the darkness of your pain, fears, and insecurities — sometimes the best you can do is just get through the day. The shadow I have referred to before can be that part of you who calls in "sick" to work because you can't bear to put on the mask of being 'fine' and you just need to stay in bed and cry.

It can be you on the day you give the finger to a driver who cuts you off, and then take out that frustration on your kid who said "Mom" a few too many times. You shout and then slam the door to your room, wondering how life can be so shitty.

You don't know what to do and you look in the mirror and loathe what you see. You feel all alone, like no one cares, and you wish you could just disappear. Before you know it, you're back in your bed, tossing and turning until the morning light gently pulls you from your restless sleep.

It's odd that you went to bed feeling worse than you had in a long time, yet as you rub the sleep from your eyes, you feel different somehow. Not great by any means, but a hell of a lot better than the day before. You hear your child coming out of the bathroom, then a soft knock at your door. They peek in to see if you're up, and you motion for them to come in. You sit up and pat your hand on the bed as a signal for them to take a seat. You take a deep breath and apologize for your behavior the day before. You admit that you took some stuff out on them that wasn't theirs to carry and wish you could go back, but you can't. You get real and say that you've been struggling a bit, although it isn't an excuse, but you hope they can at least understand a little bit and forgive you.

# CANDICE KNIGHT

Before you can finish, they reach over with a hug and tell you how much they love you and admit that they were going through some stuff as well and realized, after the fact, that they were being a little rude and had come in to apologize to you. You have tears in your eyes at this point, as I do writing this section because this is life. Life is messy and hard and complicated, even more so because we do this thing, not alone but, with a whole lot of other people who bring their own stuff into the mix and make everything even messier.

It's actually chaotic and wonderful, all at the same time. **Life is extreme sometimes, but not all the time.** The thing is that we have a lot of control over how extreme it becomes, and during the times when we don't, we just need to get through. The tornado was exactly what Dorothy in the Wizard of Oz needed to release her own armor, even though at the time she thought she had lost everything. Day by day, hour by hour, and moment by moment, you have arrived here, at this current point in your life — You made it this far. And I am so proud of you. Keep on going. Keep doing the work. No matter what you are presented with, the biggest battle often lies within. I hope you can see that for yourself by now. I just want to reassure you that no matter how often you stumble or how much doubt you have, just keep going — it will all be worth it!

This journey of shedding your armor is a testament to your courage and resilience. You've unearthed layers of self-awareness, embraced vulnerability, and faced down internal battles. Now, standing at the precipice of the unknown, it's natural to feel a little flicker of fear.

It's important to remember that the magic you seek isn't hidden somewhere "out there." It resides within you, just as it did for Dorothy. You've already faced down countless internal storms, and each challenge has brought you closer to your authentic self. It's time to embrace the unknown with open arms. Begin to see it as an invitation to explore, to grow, and to write the next chapter of your story. As you navigate the unfamiliar land-

# UNDER THE
# ARMOR

scape, trust your intuition, honor your needs, and hold onto the lessons learned along the way.

    This path may not always be smooth, but every twist and turn is shaping you into the person you were always meant to be. You are capable, resourceful, and infinitely worthy. With each step you take, the fear subsides, replaced by a quiet confidence. This journey of self-discovery is a lifelong adventure, and the best part is, you're exactly where you need to be—ready to write the next chapter filled with magic, wonder, and unwavering belief in yourself. Keep going, keep exploring, and keep believing!

## TRY THIS:
### Embrace the Unknown

The next time you feel overwhelmed by uncertainty, take a moment to breathe deeply and remind yourself of the strength and resilience you've already shown on your journey. Write down three times you faced the unknown and emerged stronger. Use these memories as a reminder of your inner power and trust that you have the capability to navigate whatever comes your way. This practice will help you embrace uncertainty with confidence and curiosity, turning the unknown into a new adventure.

Activity #16

# Chapter 17:
## Transforming Chaos into Growth and Freedom

*"The universe is transformation;
our life is what our thoughts make it."*

### — Marcus Aurelius

Embracing chaos can be a powerful way to break free from the grip of our armor. It's a journey of inviting the unknown, stepping out of our comfort zone, and releasing the need to constantly plan and strategize. Just as chaos can be uncomfortable, it is in this discomfort that we find the opportunity for tremendous growth and freedom. As we let go of the layers of armor that seek control and predictability, we open ourselves to the unpredictability of life, allowing transformation to unfold in unexpected ways. It's a process of trusting the journey, surrendering to the chaos, and discovering the strength that emerges when we release the need for constant order.

I am so excited to share this story because it just popped up right when I was planning this chapter in Guatemala. I went downstairs for a snack and stopped to chat with our yoga instructor extraordinaire. She told me how she and her partner were planning on moving to Mexico City. She's from Guatemala and her partner is from Argentina, so I asked why Mexico, and her reply was that she needed some chaos. That statement caught my undivided attention. Why chaos? She told me that life had become too predictable and she wanted to shake it up with a new adventure. What???

# UNDER THE ARMOR

My mind was spinning with an awakening that neither of us could have imagined this brief conversation would bring. I told her I had to go so I could put my thoughts on paper, and this is what I realized. As much as I was resisting, I knew that the best thing for me was not only to embrace chaos, but to invite it into my life.

I never before considered chaos as something to bring something good!

One thing I noticed is that most of my life, all I ever really knew was chaos, and I came to anticipate it as an inevitable occurrence. With chaos came a lack of control, so I just tried to make sure I had everything in order so no matter what came, I could handle it. (Can you see why I am struggling right now?)

What my yoga instructor's comment presented to me was that I was all the calm I needed in order to allow the chaos to shake free what no longer served me, so that what remained would be the keys to the doors I actually would benefit from opening. During this time of transition and transformation, it might feel uncomfortable—in fact, it should be uncomfortable. It is in our discomfort that we feel inspired to make change.

The constricting nature of our armor makes us more likely to resist change, so much so that **sometimes the Universe intervenes and sends us a reason to shift from resistance to response**. When that occurs, it can feel destructive and as if we are at the mercy of something greater than ourselves. That is always the case; we just like to believe we are in control or that if we worry or plan enough, we can make things go the way we hope. It's funny, really. If only we could see the beauty that comes from deconstructing what we have come to rely on as the way things should and can only be. All the elements of the better life we have been claiming to want can be found among the rubble. The more you let go and embrace the chaos, the stronger and more resilient you become.

Sometimes what we are resisting is leaving our old stories behind. Who are we if we don't share all the things that happened to us or that are currently happening that create chaos and upset in our lives? There is a gift in being unhappy. The payoff is that, if even for just a moment, we have someone sympathize with us. They may go home and talk about what a miserable sod we are, but in the moment of our sharing, we have their attention and their sympathy. I bet anything, though, you would tell me that you despise people feeling sorry for you. You don't want anyone's pity.

Yeah, that's your armor talking. When we share from an authentic, vulnerable state, we do so because we need compassion and care. There is nothing wrong with that. The real challenge is to realize that it's up to you to make the change, and it isn't about being stronger than you have ever been before — it's about being vulnerable and then treating yourself with kindness as you tend to your wounds and do the work that healing requires, even if that work is actually rest.

So back to my story about embracing chaos —

I had never considered that the gift I was being presented with was chaos, which is wild, since I have a whole program dedicated to being willing to open our own internal Pandora's Box. This is my interpretation of Pandora, a gal from Greek mythology who was given a gift by the Gods. They had created Pandora's box as a punishment for humankind. When given this gift, she was instructed not to open it.

Zeus, one of the Gods who had a part in her creation, had given her the gift of curiosity. As you can imagine, her curiosity got the best of her, and opening the box is exactly what she did, releasing all sorts of chaotic misfortune. She knew she had made a huge mistake, so she quickly shut the lid. Unfortunately, in her haste, hope got trapped inside. Hope is exactly what needs to be inside because I believe that's how we transform the chaos or allow it to transform us. Without hope, we can get lost.

# UNDER THE
# ARMOR

I have used this story in workshops and through coaching as a way to look at the chaos we try to keep inside because we don't want to deal with the consequences it is bound to leave in its wake. What I propose is that releasing the chaos is exactly what we need to do in order to take back our power and actually see what we've been holding on to. Never before had I seen that I have been holding chaos back when what I'm considering doing now is inviting it in.

I have done the work to create a level of calm inside myself that I never knew before. I am the calm in the eye of the wildest storm. Without that understanding and acceptance of myself, I allowed anything to make everything chaos, and I just happened to feel that I was a target. That's why I had all this armor to protect me. Who I am today is able to embrace the chaos that the universe is bringing to me, not as a form of punishment, but as a gift. I want to remove not only my armor, but also what protection looks like for me in my reality. That secure, high-paying job — protective, binding armor. My unhappy marriage brought out my armor, but was also a part of it because no matter how clear it was, we had outgrown one another — being in an intact family was a form of armor.

To truly embrace the growth and healing you now feel ready for, you're going to have to choose to step into the hurricane of change and let go of what no longer serves your higher self. Imagine yourself being transformed, shedding the heavy armor that has weighed you down. Picture this process like a caterpillar turning into a butterfly—a beautiful metamorphosis that requires more than a bit of messiness. Instead of viewing it as destruction, invite the deconstruction of the armor into your life, allowing you to see the essential elements clearly and release the rest. You are ready for this transformative journey!

Embracing chaos can be terrifying. It's a leap of faith, venturing into the unknown with no guarantee of a happy landing. But within that discomfort lies a potent fire, ready to transform you. Imagine shedding the layers of armor that have shielded you for so long. They provided a sense of safety, but they've also limited your growth. By inviting chaos, you're cracking open the armor of your fears, allowing your true self to emerge.

The process won't be pretty. There will be moments of doubt, disorientation, and maybe even a few stumbles. But with each challenge, you'll discover a hidden wellspring of resilience. You'll learn to navigate the unexpected, to trust your instincts, and to embrace the exhilarating freedom that comes with letting go.

This isn't about inviting destruction — it's about embracing the transformative power of purposeful disruption. Think of a sculptor, chipping away at the rough stone to reveal the masterpiece hidden within. Chaos is your chisel, chipping away at the armor that has held you back. Continue the journey, even when the path gets bumpy. Step into the hurricane of change, wings outstretched, ready to be reborn. This is your moment. This is your metamorphosis.

# UNDER THE
# ARMOR

## TRY THIS:
## Invite Controlled Chaos

Identify one area of your life where you feel overly comfortable or stagnant. Instead of maintaining the status quo, introduce a small, controlled element of chaos. This could be trying a new activity, changing your routine, or tackling a project you've been avoiding. Embrace the discomfort and observe how it challenges you to grow. This practice can help you break free from old patterns, ignite transformation, and discover new strengths within yourself.

Activity #17

# CANDICE KNIGHT

# RECLAIMING OUR TRUE SELF
by Moving Beyond Protection and into Self-Acceptance

# Chapter 18:
## Shattering the Armor's Grip Begins with Gratitude

*"Gratitude turns what we have into enough."*

## — Aesop

In the effort to break free from the armor that shields us, gratitude acts as a mighty force, like a hammer gently tapping away at the armor's grip. Gratitude is more than just saying, 'Thank you.' It's an amplified affirmation that chips away the tough layers, revealing the strength within. When we pause to appreciate even the small moments, we start to notice the cracks forming in our armor. It's these tiny gaps that let gratitude seep in, gradually loosening the grip of the armor. Think of it as a quiet revolution happening within, where acknowledging the good begins to shatter the protective shell. Breaking free with gratitude is the first step, a conscious choice to let the light in and weaken the armor's hold.

It wasn't actually a decision I made to create a transformation in my life. As I mentioned before, I hit an absolute rock bottom back in 2013. I remember presenting to a group of people and describing that this trek felt like something I had been on my entire lifetime. As a firstborn child in the sign of Capricorn, I was destined to tackle the most challenging trails of life, striving to reach the highest mountain peak. There was nothing I could do but take the road less traveled. By 2013, I had reached the figurative mountaintop, but the summit peak was so precarious I stumbled and came crashing down at an alarming rate.

# UNDER THE
# ARMOR

There was nothing to cushion my descent, and it certainly wasn't a graceful free fall. I bounced against the side of this jagged mountain all the way down. I was beaten and bruised, lying at the bottom, stunned and shaken to my core. It took me some time to realize that this brutal fall had actually removed many layers of my armor. I tried to get up, but I wasn't who I was when I started the trek so long ago. Because my armor had started to break away, I was left tender and raw. I had to be gentle with myself and get my bearings before I could figure out what to do next.

What came to me over the course of the next year was a set of principles that I continue to live my life by. I tell people that I didn't read about these things from any books, but each one was gifted to me from something greater than my conscious awareness. This part of my journey is the phoenix rising from the ashes, and it began with gratitude. Gratitude is my number one principle. It came to me in darkness and helped me to see the light that existed in everything all around me.

At the start, I remember feeling that I had nothing and could make a list of the things I had lost, didn't have, all the things that were wrong, the people who didn't want me, and the bleakness of the life before me until I was reminded to look at what was good. It started with my ex-husband. This was the second time we had separated and it wasn't the last. I remember feeling so much rage toward him. I felt abandoned and unloved. One day, my higher self reminded me that at one point I had loved him, and if I had loved him, married him, and chose to have children with him, then he couldn't possibly have always been as horrible as I thought he was in that moment.

I picked up a pen and in my journal wrote the things that were good about him right then. The number one thing that came to me was that he was a really good dad, or at least tried to be. He picked up our children, and they loved him. Then I recalled how he had picked up some milk for me the other day and I had appreciated that. There were so many things that were not okay between us, so many things I resented him for, but there was still something good, and that is what I chose to look at that day.

I then continued my list to include all the other things I had in my life to be grateful for. I had my children, a home, a car, a job, two dogs, friends, food — the list actually went on and on. What that list did for me was to shift my focus and choose to build on the blessings rather than dwell on the disaster. Later, I was also able to begin to look at the challenges and find gratitude for those experiences as well. When I really want to focus on gratitude, I make sure to go a little deeper and rather than just listing what I appreciate in my life, I also make sure to consider why.

The gray, drab rainy days were a great reminder of how amazing it felt to feel the warmth of the sun on my skin and to walk barefoot in the lush green grass. A rainy day was the best day to embrace heartache and sorrow. It was a time to connect to my tears and allow them to flow as a way to cleanse my soul and clear out the burdens of my heart. Thank you, rain.

Thank you to my estranged family members because even if they weren't in my life now, they had been there in the past. It took some time, but later on I was also able to be grateful for their absence from my life because I eventually realized that they weren't meant to walk with me on this next part of my journey. Later, I was able to have so much gratitude for my ex because he had taught me the lessons in self-love that — if it hadn't been for him and the numerous times we had ended, only to then be pulled back together to complete the karmic lesson once and for all — would have continued to be played out with someone else. To this day, no matter what is going on in my personal life or the world at large, I choose to believe that there is more to be grateful for than to worry about.

When I wake up in the morning and when I crawl into my bed at night, I try to remember to recount the blessings in my life that day. Have you ever been driving and got lost in your thoughts only to have your attention

# UNDER THE
# ARMOR

pulled back to the road at the most perfect time? If you had continued to be distracted, then you would have missed the light change, the car that braked suddenly in front of you, or you might have missed the street you had intended to turn down. When those moments happen, I say, "Thank you!"

There are multiple times when I notice a sign or a synchronicity and my heart is full of gratitude and appreciation. I catch sight of a deer hidden by the foliage in the forest, a friend I had been thinking about sends me a message, and a brief chat in the grocery store with a stranger provides me with a connection I hadn't known I needed. Thank you! I say thank you to the breeze as it whispers through the trees, to the toads singing in the springtime, to the snowflakes blanketing the road, and then the plows that clear it to make it safe to drive on.

What do you focus on? Can you see how gratitude is the first step to healing? It can bring you back to where you are and transform your reality if only you allow yourself to see all that you have. I was reminded of this when I longed for a new home. In my mind and to people I knew, I would think and speak about all the things I wished were different or what I desired in my new home. Then one day, I was guided to consider what my current home would say to me if it could.

It might tell me that it was hurt and maybe a little frustrated with me. It would remind me of how I felt when I first saw it and what made me decide to put an offer in. Didn't I remember how excited my husband and I were to have our very own house to raise our new family in? It was small, but cozy. The yard was beautiful with trees and perennial gardens. Didn't I love the lilac bush that I had restored back to health? When I separated from my husband, wasn't I able to manage and afford it all on my own? Wasn't the neighborhood safe, filled with amazing people, and great to go for walks through? Could I just appreciate what I had and dream about the next home without putting this one down? That's exactly the positive attitude I employed, and I continue to use it.

I have always wanted to have a cottage. My family had one in the Muskokas (in southern Ontario), and I had been going there the majority of my life. I especially loved to go alone. At one point, I had to acknowledge that I was grieving the loss of this beautiful sanctuary along with the dissociation from the family that owned it. Even if I could go back, it wouldn't be the same, because I was no longer part of the family the way I had once been. I wanted a cottage, but I told myself that I could never afford to have one. I wouldn't be able to maintain it, and no matter how I looked at it, the dream seemed impossible until I switched my way of looking at this out-of-reach desire. The first thing I did was ask myself why I wanted a cottage. What I loved about the cottage was being surrounded by nature and water. I loved the hammock between the trees and the smell of the forest all around me.

Perfect! What do I have right now? I have a house that is on a tree-lined street. In fact, my house was built in a forest, and while some trees were removed to build the homes, many, including the four on my property, were left to keep the forest alive. Just a few blocks over, I can access trails that meander through the forest that was left untouched and even continue onto the newer trails that have recently been built and can take me many kilometers in all directions. I might not be walking distance to the water, but it is so close by. There is the Detroit River, River Canard, and two great lakes! I even have a hammock hanging between the two great oaks in my private, fenced backyard. Is it possible for me to embrace and enjoy what I have access to right now and hold space for the dream that I have to own a cottage of my own someday? That's exactly what I decided to do.

Doing this also reminded me of all the things I take for granted, so one day I asked myself to imagine that if I were to wake up tomorrow with only what I was thankful for today, what would I have left? This got me thinking of all the small things we take for granted. My toothbrush, my health, hot water, clean air, chocolate chips, my fluffy pillows, access to feminine

# UNDER THE
# ARMOR

hygiene products, hugs, laughter — you get where I'm going with this. We have so much, yet we always seem to want more. Imagine showing your past self even a year ago what you have today. There is so much to be grateful for.

So, as I invite you to join me in this shift of perspective, let's cherish each moment, appreciating the seemingly ordinary aspects that make our lives extraordinary. Gratitude becomes our ally, peeling away the layers of armor we've carried for so long. If we wake up tomorrow with gratitude to guide us throughout the day, we'll find a wealth of joy in the seemingly mundane and a deep appreciation for the richness that surrounds us. With each expression of thanks, a significant layer of armor crumbles away, revealing the vulnerable yet resilient core within. Life's true magic lies not just in wanting more, but in acknowledging the abundance that already surrounds us. Embrace this practice, and watch your world transform!

**CANDICE KNIGHT**

# TRY THIS:
## Start a Gratitude Journal

Each day, take a few moments to write down three things you're grateful for. It can be as simple as a warm cup of coffee, a kind gesture from a friend, or the beauty of a sunset. Reflect on why you're grateful for each one. This practice can help you shift your focus from what you lack to the abundance that already exists in your life, gradually loosening the grip of your armor and allowing you to embrace life's richness.

Activity #18

# Chapter 19:
## Self-Awareness

---

*"We do not see things as they are,
we see them as we are."*

### — Anaïs Nin

Just as gratitude begins to crack the armor, self-awareness acts as the guiding light that exposes the intricate details of our protective shield. By willingly embracing self-awareness, we commit to peeling back yet another layer of armor, revealing the raw authenticity beneath. This principle invites us to navigate the landscape of our own expectations and perceptions to dismantle the barriers that stall our growth.

The more I paid attention to all the good around me and worked to adjust the way I viewed my circumstances, I ended up learning my second principle: being aware of my thoughts, words, actions, and expectations. Our brain processes over 70,000 thoughts per day, most of them unconscious. Imagine the impact if we became more fully aware of the information our mind processes!

While at my rock bottom, my thoughts, words, and actions toward myself became harmful and toxic. I was my own punching bag and believed I deserved the worst treatment imaginable. It took me a while to realize that I was in charge of determining my value and worth, not others.

# CANDICE KNIGHT

**My armor seemed to have left me, and I couldn't even protect myself from myself.** I was hurting myself not only inside my mind, but also in a physical way, and I swear that at some point my higher self begged me to stop. I remember telling myself that I had to be here for my kids, they needed me, they loved me. What came to me next was that I was selfish and unfair to my children. I couldn't use my kids as an excuse to get myself together. I couldn't use their love as my fuel any longer. They needed me to come back to myself because I believed I was worth it, not because I "had to" do it for them. What was the lesson I wanted to teach them? How could I hope for them to love themselves if I was treating myself with such disregard?

I remember beginning to catch myself and reflecting on what was going through my mind, coming out of my mouth or motivating my actions throughout the day. It was honestly quite overwhelming at the beginning. I remember thinking about what I had said and done and being disappointed with myself, which defeated the purpose. What I was eventually able to do was to praise myself for at least noticing. I had spent so much time living in a state of habitual practices that it was easy to feel I had no control. The fact is, that is all I had control over — myself. I no longer wanted to be a passive player in my own life, so I began to train myself to think, speak and act in a way that reflected the person I wanted to be and the way I wanted to be treated.

Remember, I'm a visual person, so I envisioned my body sitting across from me, separate but connected. I considered how she felt having my thoughts and feelings running through her mind and my words coming out of her mouth. I told her I was sorry and expressed gratitude and love. This practice felt different, more sincere. She deserved all my love.

As you pay more attention to your body, consider what it is trying to tell you. Our bodies send us messages through sensations like goosebumps and butterflies. Ignoring these signals can lead to shutdowns. Our skin, our

# UNDER THE
# ARMOR

largest and most sensitive organ, is a better defense system than the emotional armor we're stripping away.

Another visual method I like to use when I am considering the impact I'm having not only on myself but others based on my thoughts, words and actions, is to give a color and feeling to the energy I am exuding. This practice has been an easy way to tune into myself, but also as a radar for the people around me. On most days, my current color is made up of shades of pink, yellow, green, purple, and blue. They are brighter and more sparkly, depending on what I am doing, and even if they are muted and held closer rather than radiating outward, they are rarely if ever dark, foggy, clingy, and cloaked in grays, browns or black, as they were in the past because of my armor.

Think about the impression you want to leave on others. How do you want them to feel around you? What non-verbal cues do you send out? Align your thoughts, words, and actions with the person you want to be, not the part of you restricted by armor. Each day, catch yourself and reframe how you communicate with yourself. People "feel" you before they "see" you.

Begin by auditing what it is that influences your thoughts, words, and actions. What and who are you following on social media? What music and shows do you consume? Who do you spend time with? How much of these bring you joy?

**Once you change the way you see things, things you see begin to change.** Start by choosing to bring more joyful things into your life. Move into setting boundaries to preserve your precious energy. Once you pay attention to yourself, you'll notice all the ways you contribute to your own unhappiness. You don't always have control over the people and situations that influence you, but what you can begin to do is work on managing how you respond to them.

People are often looking to put the blame or responsibility somewhere else and I am not trying to tell you to blame yourself. The opposite, actually. I want you to truly see yourself and begin to treat yourself with the love, respect and protection that you have looked to others for. Stop looking to hide behind the armor that you are working to dismantle, and face the challenges with the courage to stand in your personal power. That's the hard part about transforming your life. It's up to you to make it happen, and it doesn't just happen all at once. It takes dedication, practice, and the belief that you are worth it. It also involves taking personal accountability and responsibility for what happens next.

I've come a long way in a decade. Despite stumbling, I've never returned to treating myself the way I used to. Once you see and practice these strategies, you can't go back. If you do, you aren't ready to shed that layer of armor yet. Sometimes hitting rock bottom is necessary for transformation. You have to want this change and be willing to step into the life you were destined to have.

Does this sound crazy? Maybe, but imagining amazing things happening in your life is more likely if you think positively, rather than limiting yourself. I have to remind myself daily that this life is inevitable. I'm still human, still removing my armor. Instead of worrying about the future, I'm excited about its possibilities. Perspective is everything.

When I think of the worst that can happen, I realize I've already been set up to handle it. My armor has served me well. The worst would be returning to the classroom for security. The best would be confidently moving on from my career and being unattached to what's next.

## Awareness of Expectations

Expectations are based on our perceptions of what should happen, revolving around ourselves, others, or situations. Often, they are the root

# UNDER THE
# ARMOR

cause of disagreements and resentments, if not communicated clearly. Pay attention to your reaction when expectations are met or not.

Whose idea of right or wrong is more valid? Our expectations can strip others of their individuality. Think of a time you were disappointed by an expectation you had or vice versa. How did the expectations of others have an impact on the person you are today?

I used to get upset about my husband not making the bed "properly" or folding towels my way. Eventually, I asked myself why my way was better. How was I making him feel with my critiques and redos? Once I was able to see things from his perspective, I started to tell myself to "shut the heck up" and say thank you, instead, or to say nothing at all. What a difference!!! I started to see what was really important…my husband did the laundry, folded the clothes, AND put them away.

Although there were a lot of things that contributed to our marriage not working out, I could acknowledge that there were a lot of things I hadn't been able to see while we were together. I also reminded myself that it was never his job to make me happy, nor was it mine to try to do the same for him. The more aware we are of our expectations and what lies beneath that gives them importance, the more we are better able in communicating them.

As I started to be more aware of my expectations, it changed how I communicated what I expected and helped me to listen to the expectations of others. This way of looking at things also took layers of stress off myself.

As a mom to teens, this examination of expectations is something that is a work in progress. My reaction is not solely rooted in the unfinished chores, it lies in the wound that my "I have to get it done by myself" armor is reflecting.

I ended up stopping myself from doing certain things. I would find myself getting upset, and then ask myself, "Do you want to do this right now? Do YOU need to do it?" I found that a lot of things didn't need to be done right at that moment, I didn't need to do it, and if I asked someone nicely, they might actually do it for me. I also noticed that when I didn't do anything and stopped nagging…things started to get done.

Asking myself these questions helped me to stop "shoulding" on myself. There are so many things that we think we should do or need to do. Every time you say this to yourself, next ask if this statement is actually true.

There is also the possibility that you will end up turning that 'should' or 'need' into a want. Once you decide you want to do something, it's more likely to be a positive experience. If anything, you might feel more motivated.

Self-awareness demands a commitment to paying attention to our thoughts, words, and actions. This journey isn't easy, but it's sure worth it! View challenges as self-discovery moments, for the change will surpass your expectations. You're worth the effort, and the transformation will be profound.

# UNDER THE ARMOR

## TRY THIS:
Daily Self-Awareness Check-In

Take a few minutes each day to reflect on your thoughts, words, and actions. Ask yourself:

- What thoughts dominated my mind today?
- How did I speak to myself and others?
- Did my actions and my speech align with my true self and values?

Notice any patterns or discrepancies and gently remind yourself to approach each day with more mindfulness. This practice will help you become more aware of the armor you wear and start the process of peeling it back to reveal your authentic self.

Activity #19

# Chapter 20:
## The Power in the Present

---

*"If you are depressed, you are living in the past.*
*If you are anxious, you are living in the future.*
*If you are at peace, you are living in the present."*

### — Lao Tzu

In the pursuit of unburdening ourselves from the weight of the past, the third principle directs our attention to the peace found in the present moment. Consider the mask of armor we wear that amplifies the echoes of yesterday, binding us to fragmented memories. As we explore the practice of mindfulness, we begin to notice that being fully present frees us from the constraints of both the past and the future. By being present in the 'now,' we find the best guidance for moving forward, free from the stories of our history. This principle invites you to explore the quiet power of the present, where the armor begins to loosen, offering a pathway to true liberation and a brighter, unrestrained future.

Mindfulness is a conscious reflection on the moment we are in without expectations or judgment. Being in the moment changes how you see things and how you do things because it allows you to focus on one thing at a time. I once took a mindfulness workshop, and one of the activities was to eat a raisin in a mindful manner. I just want to point out that one of the only foods I don't like is raisins. To me, they are like little fly bodies without wings. (Sorry if that visual has ruined this tasty snack for you, as well.)

# UNDER THE ARMOR

We were each given one raisin and were instructed to look at it, noticing the creases, the color, and the size. Along with noticing what the raisin looked like, we also paid attention to what it felt like. Mine was firm and wrinkly. Then we brought it close to our ear so we could hear what it sounded like when we rolled it between our fingers. Next, we put it to our noses to smell it, which is something I can admit I had never done before. Finally, it was time to put the darn thing in our mouths. We had to hold off biting into it for a moment so that we could notice what it felt like on our tongue. Next, we bit into it and started chewing this mini snack, allowing the remnants to move between our teeth, along our tongue, and eventually down our throat when we swallowed. What a process!

What I can tell you is that I had a whole new appreciation for raisins. Even though I enjoyed the taste of the one I had come to know intimately, I still wouldn't buy them at the grocery store.

I also tried being more mindful of some other activities I do habitually, which was almost like learning to do the simplest task all over again. When I brushed my teeth, washed the dishes, and made my bed, for example, I was actively involved with my mind, not just my hands. One evening, before dinner, I asked my kids to tell me what they thought went into making this meal possible.

I asked them to think about just the carrot on the plate. It was once a seed that needed soil, nutrients, and sun to grow. There was the farmer that took care of it until it was ready to be picked. There was someone involved with the processing, packaging, and delivery to the store. Someone unloaded it and got it on the shelf before I chose the product and brought it home to be cleaned, peeled, chopped, and then cooked. Finally, it was plated along with all the other parts of the meal about to be enjoyed. After all that, before the food got cold, we said a genuine 'Thank you' and acknowledged how much we have to be thankful for.

An important aspect of being in the moment is that you are able to notice things on a deeper level. When you feel out of sorts, stop for a moment and check in with yourself. Take a deep breath. (I actually like to take three.) When you are focused on your breath, you're not thinking about anything else.

It's a great way to pause and regroup so you can consider some of the following questions: What's going on? How are you feeling? Do you need something? Why are you feeling the way you are (action/situation)? Why is this not a good thing, or maybe it is a good thing? What can you do about it at this moment? What do you have control over? What's the first thing you can do to make it better or change the situation? Is this something that you could let go of? How do you do that? (I know this seems like a lot of questions but just begin with one.)

Our armor often has us worrying about what is coming next, and to alleviate that worry, we try to control the situation by making plans and anticipating all the potential possibilities. The more we get to the source of our triggers and have a better understanding of what we are truly afraid of, the better able we become at bringing ourselves back to the moment. Pause, take a deep breath, and exhale with an audible "Ahhhh…" **You are exactly where you are meant to be right now. If you weren't, you wouldn't be there.**

At the time that I am writing this book, I am not working a full-time job. At the moment I am writing this sentence, I have no idea what I will be doing once my sabbatical is over, and believe me, this is not a comfortable space to be in. I have been off for almost seven months! The first two were easy because, as a teacher, I was used to having summers off. Once classes resumed, I was looking forward to getting this book started at a retreat in Guatemala. The next thing I knew, it was November, and it felt like I needed to hurry to get the book completed.

# UNDER THE
# ARMOR

It felt different, though. I was no longer waking up to the view of volcanoes and a beautiful lake, with my meals prepared, my room cleaned, and a morning yoga lesson to get the juices flowing. I was back to getting my kids ready for school, brewing coffee in my Keurig, and getting myself to work in my office looking out my window at the barren trees and the mountain of leaves I would have to make time to rake and bag. Real life reminded me that I needed to get my butt in gear. Stress started to creep in, I began to pressure myself, and I started to make plans.

Every time I would start to think about what I would do once I had officially resigned from my career or questioned what I would do next to earn a living, I would hear a simple statement in my ear — "Write the book." This wasn't enough for me. I was going to write the book, but then what? "Write the book." No matter what I was wondering about, trying to figure out, or make sense of, I got nothing but this reminder. To be honest, that made me worry more.

I read a book once called The Surrender Experiment by Michael A. Singer, and it popped into my mind recently. The author had set an intention to surrender no matter what, in all areas of his life, and there were times when he questioned whether or not this was in his best interest. The experiences he shared seemed unlikely, yet I believe them to be true, and when I looked back on my own life, I could see all the circumstances when life would work out or take a turn for the better when I least expected it, and without any effort on my part. So why was it so difficult to do now?

I believe that the more we get under our armor, the more difficult it is to remove those oldest layers. They have been with us the longest, so they are almost a part of us. Back when I was beginning my healing journey, bringing myself back to the present moment helped me manage acute anxiety and helped me get through the day. I still need that, but this principle is guiding me in a much more significant way.

Being mindful and in the moment is also about letting go and allowing the next moments to present themselves to us. It is truly about 'being' rather than 'doing', and, for me, that is scary. Who am I if I am not doing something constructive? How can things possibly work out if I stay in the 'here and now' and simply trust that everything will work out for my highest good?

What I want you to consider is, What if — What if everything can be great? What if your armor has gotten in your way, and to get to where you feel called to be, you simply need to surrender and trust that you will get there the more you are present exactly where you are.

Deep breath here. Place your hand on your heart. Can you feel it beating? So much is happening beneath the surface. Your heart beats, your lungs expand, and your blood flows all without you doing anything.

The practice of mindfulness holds the transformative power to shed light on what truly matters and exposes the spiraling nature of our recurrent thoughts. By being present in the moment, we find a refuge from stress and anxiety, a place of calm amidst life's storms. It allows us to let go of what we can't control and embrace the power of "just being."

Remember, right now, at this moment, things are good. This can be your starting point. Take a deep breath, and begin your journey to a more peaceful, more empowered you.

# UNDER THE ARMOR

## TRY THIS:
Mindful Breathing

Take a moment to pause and focus on your breath. Inhale deeply through your nose, hold for a count of three, then exhale slowly through your mouth with an audible "Ahhhh." Repeat this three times. As you breathe, let go of any thoughts about the past or future. Simply be present in the moment, feeling the air fill your lungs and then release. This simple practice can help ground you, reduce stress, and bring clarity to your thoughts.

Activity #20

# Chapter 21:
## Nurturing Your Inner Hero

*"Kintsugi (kin-su-gi) teaches that
broken objects are not something to hide,
but to display with pride.
The art of repairing broken pottery with gold
highlights the cracks and imperfections,
embracing them as part of the object's history."*

As we peel away the layers of armor, a profound realization begins to set in. The awareness of carrying these shields for so long can evoke not just a desire to remove them, but also a sense of shame for having held onto them. Becoming more self-aware opens a window to our flaws and limiting beliefs, laying them bare before us.

To continue down this road of self-discovery and go further into the healing process, it is essential that we are gentle with ourselves. This fourth principle highlights the virtue of grace, urging us to extend compassion to the flawed person we find within. Beneath all the armor lies a brave soul, willing to face vulnerability, and embracing our imperfections becomes a testament to our strength.

We've begun to see that we are our own worst critics. We tend to look to others to be kind to us and accepting of us, yet we frequently diminish our worth. So often, we attend to the needs of others before making ourselves a pri-

# UNDER THE
# ARMOR

ority, or we feel that others are more deserving than we are. Just because we're really good at it, we don't always need to be resilient and demonstrate grit.

When we first came into this world, it was all we could do to trust those whose care we were in. We couldn't worry that our behavior—poopy diapers, crying at night—would keep them from attending to our needs or loving us. Later on, we learned to protect ourselves from the reactions of others to how we present ourselves each day. We stopped allowing ourselves to be vulnerable or to trust that others genuinely cared about us.

Our assumptions of what others think, or will think, of us cause us to compare ourselves to those around us. We often have a fear of reaching out in case we are judged or seen in an unappealing way. Our mind believes what we tell it, and what we repeat over and over again tends to manifest and form our reality. The challenging task is to catch yourself when you are being discouraging toward yourself. Pause for a moment. What did you do wrong? Was it intentional? What do you need? Can you find some grace for the you that was imperfect?

I have heard that the spiritual teacher, Matt Kahn, reminds people to love that part of themselves that: got frustrated, forgot plans with a friend, made a mistake…even when something went too far and in our minds we knew we should reign it in…it has happened and there is nothing we can do about it except to stop beating ourselves up and say, "**I love the me that….**" If not us, then who will love us and stick up for us?

When we were younger, there may have been a person that told us that it was okay when we screwed up…mistakes happen to everybody, right?! There may have been someone, though, who made us feel bad about ourselves when we did something that was seemingly wrong. There may have been some standard that we had a hard time reaching, and every time we didn't reach the bar, someone communicated to us that, in some way, we weren't good enough. And after a while we started to actually believe that crap. If we didn't, we would tell ourselves that others would probably think less of us because of our mistake, so, therefore, it still mattered no matter what we thought.

As you really make an effort to make changes in how you think and act, you will notice that you seem a little crazy. I remember that the more I noticed how often I over-thought a situation, the more I felt badly about myself and my seeming lack of control. This way of thinking defeats the purpose, don't you think?

What I ended up doing was to tell myself that at least I had caught myself, which was more than I had done previously. My worst time was in the morning before work, as I did my best to make sure my kids were ready for school. I am usually very focused on what I need to do, and in my desire to get to work on time, I tend to easily get frustrated when something or someone gets in the way of that happening the way I want it to. This frustration often turned me into a snappy bitch, which too frequently had the kids and I parting from one another in a not so positive or cheery way. I would then feel crappy and tell myself that I was a horrible mother.

I noticed that I lost my cool a lot, that I wanted to be alone a lot, and that I cried a lot. When you focus on something, it tends to seem heightened and more pronounced. I had to learn to be gentle with the person that was obviously going through something. I acknowledged the triggers, the situation, or the person and then — very deliberately, I brought myself back to the moment I was in. I would take a deep breath and do my best to be in the now, and I reminded myself that I was okay just as I was.

My 'go to' phrase, not only for myself but often for the people I work with, was that the person I was today, was exactly who I was supposed to be right now. That everything I was experiencing was helping me to grow, to heal, and eventually to be accepting and loving toward the person that I was created to be. Not everyone wants to hear this, but here is where I am,

# UNDER THE ARMOR

and this is who I am. We all have to start somewhere.

The fact that I felt that I talked too much changed to acknowledging all that I had to share with others, my willingness to be open and, eventually, I learned that there is also strength in remaining quiet and observing rather than contributing a thought to each point of discussion. The fact that I believed others felt that I spoke too quickly turned into me noticing when, in a passionate dialogue, I tended to speak faster and louder. I caught myself and gently reminded myself to take a breath and slow down, but that there was nothing wrong with what I had been doing previously.

This principle is not saying that we shouldn't take responsibility for our mistakes. But it is, instead, recognizing that we are human, flawed, imperfect, and that we are at least making an effort to be conscious of our imperfections and are willing to accept them lovingly.

If you're able to, find a picture of yourself as a child. How would you describe the little kid in the picture? Cute? Silly? Sweet? Adorable? Maybe a bit of chaos? Would you ever want that child to hear the things you say to yourself as an adult at times? How would they feel if they could overhear you? Crushed, deflated, sad, hurt? The next time you are hard on yourself or berate yourself for not doing or being better, please, remember the face of your younger self and remind yourself to be gentle, kind, loving, and accepting of the person you are. If not you, then who?

People tend to treat us the way we allow them to. We can't expect people to be understanding and accepting of us if we are not. I believe that we attract what we believe we are worth. If you want to be treated with love, adoration, and respect, you have to start treating yourself that way because if someone else tried to, you'd find a way to push that person away. Now, you might have someone you care about dearly who can be your biggest critic. Their view of you is only true if you believe it to be, and if you think that they are absolutely right in their opinion of you, but it doesn't sit right with you — then how can you use that as either an inspiration to grow or as a motivation to assert yourself and set some much-needed boundaries?

Despite how much love and compassion I have been able to extend to myself, there is still a part of me that grieves the lack of love I had growing up. Even though I can appreciate the life lessons learned from the hurt, rejection, and abandonment I felt, I can't help but long for feeling love, acceptance, and commitment from someone who is just as invested in me as I am in them. When I see examples of what I desire around me, through people I know or maybe just in a reel that comes up in my social media feed, I can choose to lament what seems to elude me or I can see these models as a confirmation that what I want is available to me. What I pay attention to and how I pay attention to it communicates a lot about what I am attracting, which reflects what I believe I am worth.

As much as I have focused on gratitude, cultivating a greater awareness of what makes me me, and being actively present in the present is what makes me able to be kinder, more compassionate, and loving to the actual woman that I am. All that I desire and dream of is absolutely meant for me, but in the meantime, I have an opportunity to continue to grow, heal, and treat myself as I want to be treated. My armor probably won't completely be gone as long as I am alive. The hourglass of lessons will continue to present me with new opportunities to elevate myself, but as long as I appreciate how far I have come and encourage myself to keep moving forward, I am more than all right.

One last thing that is important to note is that I really believe that when we are not gentle with others and cast a judgment regarding their choices, behavior, or appearance, it is actually a reflection of how we view ourselves and what our own insecurities are. I started to look at others, especially my children, and thought to myself, "I am you, and you are me." It was a life changer for me. It helped me to be directly more gentle with others and then inadvertently so, casually, even, with myself.

# UNDER THE
# ARMOR

Notice when you get all caught up with what other people are doing with their lives. In the area where I live, there was an uproar recently about gender pronouns being included as a topic in the curriculum, and that students could choose their preferred pronouns at school and the school wouldn't need to inform their parents. I was already out of the classroom when this came up, but I was aware of what was unfolding. I am curious what your immediate reaction is to this topic.

My friend and I were having a conversation about it one day, and she said that, as a parent, she would absolutely want to know. I turned to her and said that she would absolutely know because the parent that she is would have created a relationship with her child that encouraged them to communicate honestly, because, no matter what they shared, they know they would be met with compassion and a desire to understand. She wouldn't need the school to call her.

I have had many students who have chosen pronouns different from what they may have been referred to when they were born, and although it took some getting used to at times, I had no problem respecting their choices. I have raised my own children to embrace all of who they are, or at least I've done my best to reflect an acceptance and appreciation for who I am as a whole, not just the more preferable parts, and that is because of all the dedication I have made to get under my armor and love everything that has been revealed. Just be you — who else can you be?

Could you be a better version of who you are today? Absolutely! Don't fool yourself into thinking that your perfect imperfection is the end goal. What should motivate you is not to change who you are, especially not to appease someone other than yourself. A willingness to grow, heal, forgive, learn, just helps you return to the best you that has been waiting to be released from the burden of the armor you have kept hidden behind. We are all just doing the best we can with what we have, and someone on the outside can never dictate what our best is. The best on one day may not be our best on another, and that goes for everyone, so cut them some slack and love their imperfections. If you can't, then move on. Shift your focus to what brings you joy and mind your own business. I promise you, it will help you to love and accept yourself that much more.

## TRY THIS:
Self-Compassion Exercise

Find a quiet moment and look at a picture of yourself as a child. Reflect on how you would speak to that child with kindness, love, and understanding. Now, write a letter to your current self, offering the same compassion and encouragement. Acknowledge your efforts, forgive your mistakes, and celebrate your progress. This practice nurtures self-compassion, helping you to embrace your inner hero with grace and kindness.

Activity #21

# Chapter 22:
## Surrendering to the Flow

*"Sometimes you need to let go—just to see if there was anything worth holding on to."*

### — Socrates

The desire to control is like a shield we carry to protect us from our fears. We often feel the need to control things because we're afraid of what might happen if we don't. Ironically, this need for control ends up limiting our perspective, preventing us from seeing the full picture. Moreover, this control tends to dismiss the thoughts and feelings of others, leading to tension and resentment. Just as armor shields us physically, the need for control becomes a type of armor for our emotions, keeping us guarded but also preventing true connection.

What happens when things don't go according to plan? Does that mean the goal is unattainable? Is the outcome destined for doom and disappointment? Maybe we just need to embrace the desire, put it out to the universe, and pay attention to the opportunities presented to us. Things might work out better than we expected and maybe even differently than anticipated. Maybe this new way releases some of the stress that accompanies a well-intentioned plan and will flow according to a plan designed by the Divine.

Letting go of control is about surrendering, which is one of the most difficult things to do when you have armor keeping you from letting go. **When we surrender, we stop fighting and resisting**. We allow things to happen rather than trying to make them happen. We stop getting in our own way and let others find their way. What are we afraid will happen if we let go of control? What's the worst that can happen? Why is that so bad?

What does control do to us? To others? How does it make us feel? When I was going through this stage—still am, to be honest—I was really stressed and anxious. I was snappy and irritable. I have heard that those who had very little control growing up cling to it desperately later on in life. I am not sure if this is a proven fact, but it definitely fits for me. Khalil Gibran (world famous Lebanese philosophical writer) stated that **our anxiety doesn't come from thinking about the future, but from wanting to control it**. Hmmm…good point.

While writing this book, I can honestly say that I struggled with feeling that I had no control. More than anything, I wished for a guarantee that I was on the right track and that the next steps on my path would be revealed in a clear and obvious way. I have never been more anxious about my choices than I have been since I began my sabbatical from my career with the intention for it to lead to my resignation. I think it's because everything I have been practicing over the course of a decade — to become more self-aware and free myself from the shackles of emotional armor — has prepared me for this exact moment.

My marriage ended, and four years later, I am thriving because it's over. I decided to leave my teaching career, and, although I have big dreams, there's still a part of me that is afraid to trust that they will actually become reality. When moments like this happen, I can ask myself what I have control over right now, and the answer is to keep moving forward. **There is no going back.**

# UNDER THE
# ARMOR

When I think about what is under my fears, it all goes back to having and providing security. I know that I could return to the classroom, but that is a big no. So I take a deep breath every single time I find myself in this mindset, and I reassure myself that I'm okay. My life is okay, and I can either continue worrying or take a look around, let go, and see what unfolds next. Haven't things always ended up working out better than expected? Maybe not at the beginning, but eventually they do…I mean, look where I am right now.

The ego, often seen as our conscious mind, acts as a form of armor, shaping and defining our personality over time through life experiences. Just as armor shields the physical body, our ego shields our emotions and thoughts, coloring our view of the world. Each person's unique set of experiences and beliefs forms the lens through which they see life. The same situation can be interpreted in a multitude of ways, demonstrating how our individual armor filters our understanding of the world around us.

Our ego can be a great companion, but it isn't always the best guide. It is more like an annoying backseat driver, and I am glad that I have learned how to notice it and quiet it so I can tune in to a deeper knowing that I can trust, which is my intuition. Initially, I had to be pretty firm with my ego. It really wanted to run the show, and with so many thoughts running through my mind, creating a multitude of stories which lead to some pretty dramatic reactions, I had to be vigilant so that I could shut it down before it got carried away.

What does letting go look like? This was the F- - - It Stage for me. Saying "f- - - it" helped me to see that the things I thought were a big deal were often not my concern at all. It helped me to ease up on others and, more importantly, on myself. This was so helpful and relevant during Covid! All the waiting we had to do in getting basic supplies, and then the essential service providers, feeling the need to apologize for the situation that was way beyond their control, and their pay scale, was a great reminder to take stock of what I had control over and how I wanted to respond to the lack of control that was affecting the entire world. I would ask myself, 'What do you have control over right now? Do you need to say or do anything at this moment? Can you just be patient?' F- - - it! Let that sh*& go!

Before I was aware of my controlling nature, I made the decision to enroll my children in a full French education system. Their father was hesitant, initially, since neither of us spoke the language, and he was concerned we wouldn't be able to assist them with their learning. In my mind, this was the best thing we could do for them. I had a feeling that each time my child asked me for help, I would become a teacher, rather than a mom, and no child needs that. The funny thing is that my children excelled without me micromanaging them. There is a lesson that I can see only now that I am aware of the need to release control in so many areas of my life and those who happen to be on my radar, such as my children, my friends, my extended family. Things will continue to proceed with or without me having a say.

The results of letting go of control have been astounding. I am able to focus more on what is actually important, and I realize how much of what I had previously paid so much attention to was actually very unimportant. I have a lot less on my plate. It has allowed me to have more trust that the universe would take care of me and of everyone else. I even told my children that I was simply a guide, here to show them what I thought was a good way to live life, but that, in the end, they had to make decisions for themselves and sort out the consequences, good or bad, of those choices.

I had a friend over the other day, and she told me that she was going to get a large settlement from an injury she sustained on a rental property. She was still waiting for surgery more than a year after the

# UNDER THE
# ARMOR

accident, and her mobility was greatly impacted. Along with that there was pain, financial impact, and the potential of long-term disability. After she left, I realized something major for myself. If I didn't stop focusing on a lack mentality about my ability to provide adequately for my children, then I could very well end up finding myself in a similar situation.

I'm not saying that she asked for this accident to happen to her, but there is some truth to the idea that we attract what we put out — or we attract what we broadcast unconsciously/consciously out to the Universe. If I am constantly focused on what I don't have, or if I believe that what I desire is impossible to achieve, then that negative vibration is what my mind and my personal energy are likely to be putting out to the universe, and I will continue to see and attract those less than ideal experiences in my life.

I could relate to this friend because, even though I was financially secure after the death of my mother, my financial security somehow seemed finite to my subconscious, emotional mind — and a negative, lack mindset took hold of my subconscious. It didn't seem to register that after all those years, long after my inheritance had run out, I had always had more than enough financial security. Why was it so challenging for my subconscious mind to trust that financial security would continue?

I met with a financial advisor to discuss my plans to leave my career. I had actually put this conversation off for months because I was afraid of what they might say. I was concerned that I would have to justify my choice, and that I would be judged as crazy or selfish. Instead, I received valuable insight, options, and a plan that will set me up comfortably as I establish myself in my future financial endeavor. I left that appointment feeling safe. That was the first thought that came to me. With all this factual information laid out before me, I realized that there was no way I could ever bring up money as a reason to be afraid. Everything was going to be fine, and I needed to shift my attention to what mattered.

Can you consider that everything is just as it should be? If we resist, we won't know of the insights from our mistakes or the lessons we have an opportunity to learn from. If we release control and trust that life is happening for us so that we can learn, grow, heal, and flourish then we will get so much more out of the experience. Today, try to let go just a little more than you did yesterday. It will feel weird, and you'll notice the feelings it brings up. You have been getting ready for this, shedding layers of armor along the way.

Go back to gratitude for what you have, become aware of your triggers and needs, and bring yourself back to the moment with some deep breaths. Ask yourself some reflections to gain clarity on the source of your fears, and then be gentle with yourself. Remind yourself of the days when you were responding from a person speaking from an armored perspective. Look how far you have come.

Letting go of control can feel terrifying, like stepping off a ledge with no guarantee of a soft landing. But within that fear lies immense power. By surrendering the illusion of control, we open ourselves to a universe brimming with possibilities. We discover a wellspring of resilience within, and a trust in the unfolding journey of life.

Imagine yourself, lighter and unburdened by the weight of control. You're present in the moment, empowered by your intuition, and ready to embrace the unexpected adventures that await. Take a deep breath, release your grip, and begin your transformation today.

# UNDER THE
# ARMOR

## TRY THIS:
## Release Your Grip Exercise

Find a quiet place and take a few deep breaths to center yourself. Close your eyes and visualize a tight grip you have on a situation or outcome. Picture yourself slowly opening your hand, releasing the need to control. As you do this, repeat to yourself, "I trust the process and allow things to unfold as they are meant to." Practice this visualization daily to reinforce the habit of letting go, embracing the flow of life with trust and openness.

Activity #22

# Chapter 23:
## Freedom Through Forgiveness

*"To forgive is to set a prisoner free
and discover that the prisoner was you."*

### — Lewis B. Smedes

Forgiveness is freedom. When you choose to forgive someone, including yourself, you begin to free yourself from the restraints of resentment, anger, and regret. Sometimes, forgiving someone is easier said than done, and more times than not, it can be a process rather than a one-time declaration. Our emotional armor provides reasons not to forgive, reminding us that letting go puts us at risk of being hurt again. By getting under the armor, we shed parts of ourselves that no longer exist in the present moment. The past cannot be changed, but here we are standing in our truth, able to reclaim the power we have given to someone else, which has kept us trapped for far too long.

Sometimes you have to forgive someone who has no intention of ever apologizing or taking responsibility for their actions. Some of these people you can release from your life completely and focus on healing the wounds left in their wake. Others are difficult to forgive, and even if you do, they remain in your life, creating new reasons for you to question why you forgave them in the first place. If you are truly able to forgive, you will find the next step is to create clear, firm boundaries in all your relationships moving forward.

# UNDER THE ARMOR

I imagine shadows of our past selves lingering inside us, trapped beneath our emotional armor. They are remnants of who we once were, stunted and frozen in time due to an experience we haven't moved past yet. These parts still wait for acknowledgment, validation, or an apology, and eventually, it is up to us to do that for ourselves, even if no one else will. These shadows keep our armor in place, and until we revisit them with an intention of forgiveness in our hearts, they will remind us of how we were wounded.

I have practiced seeing these parts of myself and giving myself permission to feel whatever came up. After diminishing myself or stewing in anger for so long, I was finally able to acknowledge that my feelings were absolutely okay. I could see my contribution to the situation, even if all I did was enable someone who ended up hurting me. I then asked myself what I could do right now to make it better. Did I need to express it out loud to someone? Did I need to write it down? Did I need to confront someone and speak my truth? What would be the consequences? **Whatever I chose to do, I had to do it with no expectations about what might happen next**. I was doing this for myself, regardless of the reaction of the other person or people involved.

When you confront someone with your heart free from armor, it's important to consider how you communicate with them. If you start by blaming them for your misery and unload a whole bunch of wrongs they have done to you, not much good will come from that. Anyone would get defensive. Focus on yourself first. When you start to heal, you are bound to see things differently, you are more empowered to speak your truth, and there are times when you realize that it is in your best interest not to bother saying anything at all.

Forgiveness is not a one-time thing. It's not as easy as saying, "Okay, I am done with this, and I release the hold this experience or person has had on me." If it is significant, it may need to be revisited over time.

You will know by how long you have held onto a hurt or injustice and how often the story replays in your mind. Certain experiences leave tendrils that extend past the event. You can never really be prepared for when they might wrap around your heart and tug, reminding you of the pain attached to a particular person and memory.

Forgiveness is about being in the moment. Sometimes something triggers a painful memory, and you allow it to build and build as every wrong ever done to you comes to the surface. When you catch yourself experiencing this flood of feelings, you can choose to stop the mind chatter and ask yourself, 'What is bothering me right now? What is at the root?'

I once signed up for a forgiveness workshop because I wanted to forgive someone I had loved dearly. I felt hurt by them and wanted to move on, which meant forgiving even without closure. What I got from that workshop was completely different from what I had expected. The facilitator introduced the group to Ho'oponopono, a Hawaiian practice of forgiveness, meaning "to make right." The idea is that **we are 100% responsible for everything we experience.** It is based on the power of love, gratitude, and the practice of letting go and letting Go(d).

The Ho'oponopono mantra is:

- I'm sorry,
- Please forgive me.
- Thank you.
- I love you.

During the workshop, the facilitator asked participants to imagine a version of ourselves seated in an empty chair across from us. We recited the Ho'oponopono mantra in our heads, completing each thought with whatever needed to be expressed. I don't remember exactly what I said

# UNDER THE
# ARMOR

to my unarmored self, but it was something like this: "*I'm sorry*, Candice, for putting so much pressure on you and holding you responsible for things that weren't yours to figure out. *Please forgive me* for putting you down and making you feel unworthy of love and belonging. *Thank you* for not giving up. *I love you so much.* You are a loving, resilient, compassionate person, and you deserve all the happiness in the world." At that moment, I had a clear vision of my mother coming up to me, wrapping her arms around me, and saying thank you. She told me she had been waiting for me to understand. That vision incited a flow of tears, and something big shifted inside me. It felt like another layer of my armor had been removed.

Practicing this principle has helped me genuinely forgive people. You can start by seeing the person beyond the filter of your armor and outside the role they play in your life, like mother, husband, or friend. Every person, no matter their role, is simply doing the best they can with the armor they bear. When you can separate them from their role in your life, you can see the relationship differently and recognize that it isn't really about you.

When I was ready to forgive my father, I tried to imagine who he was as a person. The image of him as a six-month-old baby, smiling for the camera, came to mind. I mentioned before that my grandmother had not been able to hold her first born child, my father, until he was three years old because she had tuberculosis. My grandfather did his best to care for my father, but for most of the day my father was watched over by someone who was not his mother. I imagine that these early years of life began the creation of my father's own emotional armor.

Once my grandmother was healthy and out of quarantine, I'm sure there was a lot to get used to. How did this transition affect my toddler father? I'll never know, but when I imagine my father's healing journey, it seems it would go all the way back to the beginning of his life. Does facing many challenges excuse his later behavior? No, but it helped me see him as a person, just like me, and after some time and reflection, I had compassion for him, which allowed me to forgive him. I just wanted to be free of the way the memories of him made me feel, and that was up to me.

I spoke to my dad just before going to Guatemala to write this book. I told him I wanted this book to help people who had grown up having to be strong and resilient. I also let him know that this was part of healing the generational trauma that has impacted my life in so many ways. I believe the deep wounds of my family that I am committed to healing as they show up in my life today will spare my children from having to heal them down the road. They will have their pains, and they may need to forgive me for any hurt I unintentionally caused. The more I forgive people in my life, acknowledge my wrongdoings, take responsibility, and apologize with the intent to do better, I show my children that we are all just people doing the best we can today. It says a lot about your integrity and willingness to be your authentic self outside your armor when you ask for forgiveness and are willing to forgive.

My hope is to limit the trauma I might pass on to another generation if I fail to do the work to heal myself. **The more we heal, the bigger the ripple effect**. My healing and willingness to forgive my father has also helped him heal, though that was never a concern of mine. I learned that he had blamed himself for more than thirty years following the death of my mom and brother. I had forgotten he was supposed to pick us up for the remainder of the Christmas holiday. He continued to tell himself that if he had been a better father, the accident would never have happened.

For all that I had to forgive him for, him being the reason for the accident had never crossed my mind. I told him nothing could change

# UNDER THE
# ARMOR

what happened, and I hoped he could forgive himself, not for the accident, but for not being the father my brother, sister, and I needed. I told him I had blamed myself when I was in the hospital. Why hadn't I asked to go to the bathroom before we left? I thought that if I had delayed us a little, the accident would never have happened. The thing is, sh&% happens. Sometimes it's really bad, and there are times when, if we had made a different choice, there might have been a different outcome, but here we are, with what did happen, and there is nothing we can do to change it.

After forgiving my father, a new relationship with him was forged where I can set boundaries and say how I feel. I am no longer a child — I am an adult and present myself as such. The family member I had taken the workshop to forgive is no longer in my life. I did forgive him later on, but I also made the decision to move on. Doing this work with these significant people helped me through my final separation and divorce from my husband. Although I have forgiven him, I have only recently discovered how to get from under the layers of emotional armor tied to my story associated with him.

When we feel hurt, we hold onto anger, and I didn't want that with my ex. I wanted to move on and cultivate a respectful co-parenting dynamic for the sake of our kids. I chose to be thankful for the lessons I learned from him, the most important being what I desired in a future relationship and what I would never accept again. I hoped he would be the final lesson when it came to attracting healthy, unconditional love. I was grateful for our three children, and I can say with 100% certainty that this mindset helped me manifest the most amicable divorce possible.

I still believe in the idea that, 'I am you, and you are me.' This way of thinking has helped me because if we are all connected, then the negative energy we put out in anger affects not only them, but us as well. It also creates a ripple effect and impacts anyone who crosses our path. I remember hearing that **every action is either an act of love or a call for love**. An act of love makes us feel good. A call for love, if not shared in a healthy way, can look and feel angry or bitter. What does the person who hurt you need most right now? What is making them tick? This is when I choose to send out love and light, or maybe it is just nothing at all. In the end, I want the person to be happier in their life because that is the energy I want connected to me.

Even though I appreciate that we are all connected and truly desire that each person on the planet finds joy and peace, I also know it is not up to me to make that happen. In fact, I can't make it happen because, just like myself, every person has their own choices to make and their armor to get under to heal. At some point, we need to release attachment to the outcome of another person's journey, no matter how much we care or how much potential we see in them. I no longer want to drain my joy and peace to boost someone else's levels. I can forgive someone and see the pain behind their motivation, but that doesn't make me responsible. The best I can do is see people for who they are, remove what doesn't serve me, or set a clear boundary and stay true to myself first and foremost.

One thing that has helped me heal and forgive more freely is that before we came into this human incarnation, our souls made a plan for our lifetime. Other souls made arrangements to play certain roles in our lives. These plans were made so that we could learn certain lessons from each other. I don't believe bad things happen to us as punishment. Karma is not about bad things happening because you did something wrong. To me, karma is all about the lessons we need to learn to return to our core essence. **Things keep repeating in our lives until the lesson is learned**. Does that make as much sense to you as it does to me?

I believe that if we can ask ourselves what we could learn from the

# UNDER THE
# ARMOR

experience, the lesson might help us move through grief or anger and into forgiveness. We can remind ourselves that there is nothing we can do to change what happened. We can't erase how it made us feel or make the person say sorry or make amends, but we can heal and move forward. After all, forgiveness is for ourselves, not for the other person.

I'm not trying to convince you to agree with "everything happens for a reason," but you have a choice to look at what happened as something that happened for you rather than to you. Why does it matter? It shifts the narrative from one of a victim to one capable of not only surviving but thriving despite the challenges faced. This is very difficult when you have been victimized. Yes, there are things that happened that should never have happened, but they did. So now what? How can you take those stories and shift the narrative so you can get under the armor that you used to protect yourself during those experiences?

Where do you want to go now? Do you want to continue to carry those heavy emotions with you, or can you take a look at yourself as a hero on a journey? You made it this far. Today, you can look at those aspects of yourself stuck beneath the armor and free them from the stories you insist on retelling. Show them how far you have come, that, despite what happened in the past, you made it here, and through forgiveness you can move on. The choices you make now can shift your reality to one of your making. It is not easy by any means, but it is worth it because you are worth it and always have been. You need to let go of the past so you can move freely into the future, little by little, step by step — as long as you're here, you're right where you're supposed to be, and you're right on time.

## TRY THIS:
Forgiveness Visualization

Close your eyes and take a few deep breaths to center yourself. Picture a person you wish to forgive, including yourself, sitting across from you. As you breathe in, silently say, "I'm sorry." As you exhale, say, "I forgive you." Continue this for a few minutes, feel the emotions and begin to release resentment and allow compassion to fill the space where anger and hurt once resided. Repeat this practice daily to foster forgiveness and healing.

Activity #23

# Chapter 24:
## The Gift of Giving

*"I am open and receptive to
all the good and abundance in the universe."*

### — Louise Hay

Our emotional armor often extends beyond protection from external threats — It creates a shield against the act of giving, both to others and to ourselves. This layer of armor, designed to safeguard us from perceived scarcity, ironically binds us to a mentality of lack. When we operate under the fear of not having enough, it becomes a self-fulfilling prophecy that restricts our ability to be generous. As we remove the armor of scarcity, we uncover the liberating truth that **generosity generates abundance.**

I learned about being generous and making myself my number one priority when I noticed that I always seemed to hesitate when deciding about whether or not I should do or buy something nice for myself. I would ask myself if I really needed it, and more often than not I would talk myself out of it. It always seemed that someone else's needs were more important than mine or that something else was more essential. I often made choices based on practicality. I'll never forget the first few things I chose to do without caring about what anyone else would think and without second guessing my decision.

The first thing was getting my tattoos. At 39 years of age, I decided to get two tattoos on the same day. Not really a big deal but it was something that I had been putting off for ages. The images I chose were miniscule. The total cost was $100.

You might wonder how getting a tattoo connects to generosity. It was about being generous to myself without worrying about others' opinions. No one told me I shouldn't get one, but there was a part of me that wondered how I would be viewed, especially because I was a teacher. Even though $100 wasn't much, it felt frivolous, especially as a newly single person focused on family finances. But I learned that doing something for myself didn't need justification. Each prick of the needle weakened the foundation of my emotional armor, strengthening my soul underneath.

The next, much more significant thing was my decision to go to Jamaica with my children. It was quite a costly adventure, but also a once-in-a-lifetime opportunity. I remember dipping into my children's education fund to help cover the cost of the flights. I had to remind myself over and over again that doing so was okay, that this trip was a learning experience in itself. This trip ended up being one of the best decisions I had ever made, and it was the beginning of many more opportunities to be generous with myself, which led to me being more open to being generous with others.

In the past, I would make sure others approved of my choices, almost like seeking permission. I am not sure what it was that made it become easier to treat myself to things I wanted. I think that I would ask myself if it was something I really wanted, and if the answer was yes, I would loosen the reins and take a chance on myself. I began to notice that these decisions to be generous with myself brought more than I had bargained for.

# UNDER THE
# ARMOR

These choices brought me new connections, learning opportunities, and experiences that started to shift my reality and helped me to level up out of limitation and lack, to abundance and brilliance. The biggest investment came in 2019 when I invested over $12,000 in a coaching program to grow my business so that I could begin to transition out of my career as a classroom teacher.

I'd discussed leaving my career with my husband, who didn't seem to oppose it, but later claimed it was the reason he left. The day prior to this fateful weekend, I had arranged for a financial advisor to come speak with us about how we could move forward financially prepared. I remember him being preoccupied, but he agreed to do what he could to support my decision, and then he said that he had to head to his parents so he could help out his brother. The financial advisor left soon after. I felt inspired, and then I headed out the next day to Toronto for a weekend conference hosted by the people running the coaching program I was about to invest in.

It was such a powerful weekend, and I was pumped to move forward with my dream. I had even splurged and gotten myself business class tickets for the train ride home. I had noticed that my husband had been pretty distant all weekend, but I figured he had his brother on his mind, and I was so happy that I didn't let it get me down. When he arrived late to pick me from the train station and then proceeded to speak to me in a way that seemed off, I quickly came down off my energy high.

What I was absolutely not prepared for was what happened next. Later that night we had a heated conversation out in the car to avoid upsetting the kids. He then got out of the car, and after a good cry I went into the house and up to our bedroom. He opened the bedroom door at some point, looked at me, but didn't say anything, and then he closed the door. The next thing I knew, I heard his car start, and he drove off.

Even though he had told me as we spoke in the car that he felt we weren't connected anymore, I thought he was just pissed and wanted to cool off over at his parents house. It was my troubled son who told me the next morning after I had asked him what was bothering him that his dad had told him and his sister that he was leaving the family. What??? That was it. He never came back. Now what does all this have to do with being generous? I'm getting to that.

After the initial shock, I questioned my $12,000 investment. I considered asking for a refund, but ultimately decided to continue. This decision was monumental for me, as financial security had always been my biggest concern. In the end, I recouped most of the investment through my tax return. Although the program didn't pan out as expected, I gained invaluable insight: I am worth the investment, and things work out, not in spite of treating myself, but because I did.

Since that time, I have invested in other coaching and educational programs, lessons, activities and even more expensive adventures, such as Mindvalley University in Estonia for three weeks, and then the following year in Guatemala to write my book! Nothing has been a waste, but each time that I have been generous with myself it has helped me to expand and evolve in ways I could never have imagined. I have met amazing people, and they have opened doors to me that I would never have had access to had I not made myself a priority. What I decided was to stop resisting, because I no longer wanted to focus on what I had to lose, instead, I put my mind on what I potentially had to gain!

Reflecting on my upbringing, I see how my beliefs about money shaped my reluctance to be generous with myself. Raised by a single mother, I learned that money was for "important" things like bills, not for personal desires. This reinforced my armor of self-denial. However, as I began honoring my worth, I became happier, and so did my children. **Generosity is tied to happiness, health, and life satisfaction.**

# UNDER THE
# ARMOR

I am a responsible person, and nothing I was doing was being done to fill a void, like some people do when they go shopping just to shop and buy a bunch of things they can't afford or don't even want. There are so many ways our limiting beliefs impact our spending habits and our generosity to ourselves and to others. For me, being generous to myself was about honoring my worth. The more I did these things, the happier I became and, in turn, the happier my children became. It is a fact that people who are generous are happier, healthier, and more satisfied with life.

When we are doing too much and not taking time for ourselves or giving to ourselves, we will inevitably become resentful, but that is on us. We need to learn to say no when we are asked to do something we can't or don't want to do. It's okay — to — say — no. There are consequences to every decision, so we have to be ready to accept what might come with the choice, but that is no different than the consequences that come along with saying yes. Stop feeling guilty or selfish about making yourself a priority.

Once you give to yourself on a more regular basis and feel good about it, you will feel that it becomes easier to give to others, and you'll find that more abundance comes right back to you. **Money is an energy, and energy must flow!** Embrace the idea that there is more than enough for everyone.

I feel like we are living in a time where people feel the need to covet things to themselves because they fear that there will not be enough for them to be happy in life. Embrace the idea that there is more than enough for everyone. If ever we are struggling, there will actually be help right around the corner if we are open to receiving. When you focus on lack, that tends to be all that you see and when you believe that, you often will find yourself surrounded by others who believe the same, which just leads to a bunch of venting and complaining instead of attracting abundance.

I know I have said this before, but "I am you and you are me." When you give to someone, do so without any expectations. If you recall, it is our expectations that cause our misery. When you give, do so because you want to do something good regardless of what you will get in return. If you hold the door for someone and they don't say thank you, please don't say in a snarky way, "You're welcome!" Just remind yourself that you did something nice because you wanted to.

Do things with good intention, and that's all that matters. That "pass it on" expectation at the drive thru is way too much pressure and not at all what being generous is all about. You should not feel guilted into giving. It's okay to say no.

Allowing myself to be generous helped me to loosen the bonds of my armor. Inadvertently, getting those tiny tattoos was the beginning of me putting myself first. I came to see myself as number one! No longer did I put what I thought everyone needed ahead of my own. I stopped telling myself that my needs were selfish, frivolous, and unimportant. There is empowerment in making yourself a priority, and the impact it has on others, especially the people you care for, is beyond measure.

Generosity should not be measured by expectations. No relationship is 50/50, nor should it be. If you find yourself penny-pinching or splurging recklessly, reflect on how your armor is blocking the freedom found in balancing giving, saving, and spending. As you chip away at your armor, you release limiting beliefs and tune into your soul's truth. Start today by giving generously—your time, talents, or a kind word. You'll be amazed at how much joy it brings, not just to others, but to yourself.

# UNDER THE
# ARMOR

## TRY THIS:
## Small Acts of Generosity

Start by practicing small acts of generosity each day. Buy a coffee for the person behind you in line, donate a few items to a local food bank, or spend a few minutes helping a colleague with a task. Notice how these small acts make you feel and how they shift your perspective on abundance. Embrace the joy and fulfillment that comes from giving, and watch how it transforms your outlook on life.

Activity #24

# Chapter 25:
## Safety in Surrender

*"Intuition is a spiritual faculty and does not explain, but simply points the way."*

## — Florence Scovel Shinn

The journey of removing layers of armor — more or less, surrendering — has revealed something profound: There is safety in surrender. As we drop our protective shields, we create space to sense, to give in to, and to trust our intuitive guidance. It's like stepping into the vast unknown with a newfound confidence instead of hesitating on each next step. In surrendering the need for excessive control through our psychological armor, we discover an inner peace where our instincts become a guiding force. This becomes a symbol of our innate strength.

I hinted at the fact that my journey included a spiritual aspect to it. I have told people that I am on the spectrum of academics and the "woo-woo" ("spiritualism"). When Reiki was introduced to me back in 1998 while I was studying massage therapy, I thought it was stupid. I mean, massage therapy made sense because it was medically based, but energy healing—give me a break! Turns out, 20 years later, I became a Reiki master and actually realized that even as a massage therapist, my ability to connect to people's energy was apparent, and I was using it in my practice without being aware of it.

# UNDER THE
# ARMOR

I have always been connected to Spirit, but I never questioned it or even explored it. I'm not going to get into all the ways I am connected to the spirit world, because that's not what this topic is about. What I want to invite you to consider is the importance of connecting to your own higher self and your intuition through surrendering your armor, giving it up to go within. I encourage you to imagine the idea I introduced previously: that we are all on a journey of the soul and that each of us decided before we came into this world what this lifetime would be like.

Hear me out, for a moment.

What if my soul decided to be a woman of color, my parents asked if I would be okay with having them guide me this time around, and maybe they even cautioned me that it wasn't going to be an easy time? As an energetic soul, I was brimming with enthusiasm and not worried in the least. I was already aware of the amazing people who would show up in my soul circle along the way as friends, lovers, mentors, and even haters. Until I got underneath my human-experience related armor, I wouldn't initially see them as valuable helpers, but that was all part of the Divine plan. Everything was going to be an unfolding of all the lessons I had signed up for, and I was ready and willing.

Then I was born and, even though this 'knowing' was there, I forgot it. We all did, although some remember earlier than the rest of us. Others sadly hold so tight to their human ego side, aka their armor, that they never have an awareness of their soul's true journey.

Now, maybe this is all BS—but who knows for sure about much in life, anyway? This belief, which keeps getting more beautiful the more I grow, is what helps me to let go and embrace the possibility of just about anything. Why not? Humans are created from a sperm and an egg and, even if we happen to be identical in appearance—twins of the same biological material—we are so unique in who we are as a personality. Why do we need to shut down the magic and mystery of life? Why do we stop ourselves from dreaming and believing in things we can't possibly prove?

Does it make more sense to believe that everything and everyone over the course of your life has just been a random coincidence? Have the good times and the more challenging ones simply happened to you rather than for you? These beliefs are what have contributed to all the layers of armor that you continue to hold onto. But when you shift your way of thinking and surrender to the possibility that you are actually a co-creator of your life story, things begin to change, and you can see that each experience in life is a lesson that has taught you something valuable and contributed to your growth.

Once you see things differently, you are no longer a pawn in the game of life. You become a player with opportunities to "spin the wheel" and then choose which way to go next. When you allow yourself to go within and trust the guidance of your soul, you will find that the adventure ahead moves more seamlessly. Your armor is no longer able to create resistance or freeze you in fear, making life choices more difficult than they need to be. There truly is safety in surrender to the unknown, but you have to let go of your armor to find out.

We all have access to our inner, Intuitive Voice. It's often muffled beneath our armor and, as long as we hold onto our armor and aren't prepared to listen, it doesn't have much to say. To me, this Voice is like a butterfly fluttering in and passing you by, if you don't pay attention. The ego-fueled voice is what we all know and love. It gets us motivated and also makes us scared of the unknown. It's like a crow cawing loudly, although its message can only be heard in our conscious mind. We hear it, we listen, and we analyze it. If we don't check it every now and then, it can get a little out of control, and we start ignoring the softer

# UNDER THE ARMOR

voice of our intuition that resides in us all.

The soft Voice of your Intuition is always available, and even if you think you haven't heard it yet, you have, and you have probably even listened to it a time or two. It's an inner knowing, sometimes a feeling you get in your gut. It could be what people call a coincidence, although I don't believe anything is actually random. The more you pay attention and surrender the layers of armor, the more clear the coincidences and meanings become.

Before I even knew about this inner, knowing part of me, I was connected, and I can see, looking back, just how guided I was. I have so many examples that I'd love to share, but I'll stick with just one. Sometimes you don't know why, but you feel you must do something. Have you ever looked back and wished you had listened to your gut? It's scary sometimes, isn't it? Trust me, I know.

I had been wanting to leave teaching for a while. I loved teaching and my students, but I just outgrew the way things are required to be delivered in education. The first time I planned on leaving teaching, I got pregnant despite my husband's vasectomy, and along came my unexpected baby—at the age of 42! The Universe was saying, 'Yeah, not yet. There's more to do.'

The next time I got all excited to leave teaching was right before my husband left me and I felt, 'Damn — really??' The Universe just encouraged me to be patient. My time was coming, but there was still more to do. Guess what?? The time is now, and I have been scared and fearful, doubtful, and my desire to control the outcome still creeps up every so often. I know, I know — I said all this great stuff and showed you how far I have come in getting under all that armor I have been carrying for as long as I can remember But here I am, at the threshold, parachute on, yet hesitating to jump. I'm doing it, though. I am going to face my fear as I had every single time before, and I am going to do it again. You know why this time it is so scary? It's because I have done the work, and I know it's not all random. I believe, without a doubt, that I am co-creating all this awesomeness as a partner with the Universe.

The majority of the decisions I made throughout my life had been influenced by my armor because I was so burdened by the layers of armor my trauma had accumulated. Despite that, there was also a part of me that was connected to my Spirit, so that the whispers of my soul didn't fall on deaf ears. Whether it was because I survived that accident so long ago, to be without parents and have to rely on myself or maybe it is just in my nature to listen to the guidance from within. Whatever the reason, I am so grateful.

I may not know what is next, but I do know that I am not meant to stay here, in the city I have lived the last 30 years, any longer. The career I established is over, my marriage I fought long and hard to maintain is over, and my older kids have moved out. I found a sense of belonging in this community, but I don't think it will bring me to the next level of my soul lessons.

For the sake of everything I have done, not just getting under my armor, but removing as much of it as possible so that I can finally surrender and trust in my soul path, I have to move on. If I were to stay—and the only reason would be to maintain a routine of daily consistency and familiarity for the sake of my youngest child—I would actually be denying her the best parent I could possibly be.

Right now, I have no idea what is next, but I am going to take my own advice, and I'm going to take that leap of faith, because I no longer believe that I will crash and burn on the descent into the unknown. When you decide to take an intuitive leap like I have, you are going to experience some bumps on the way because there's still armor left for

# UNDER THE
# ARMOR

you to work through. What you have now is a parachute to help you glide and go further than you ever could believe possible. You are about to level up and begin the biggest adventure yet on your inner hero's journey, free from the burdens that have brought you to this moment and prepared you for the next. Now that you have surrendered, and are ready to tune into your intuition, you are finally ready.

## TRY THIS:
Trusting Your Intuition

Take a moment each day to quiet your mind and tune into your intuition. Start by sitting in a comfortable position, closing your eyes, and taking a few deep breaths. Ask yourself a simple question about your day or a decision you need to make, and then listen for the subtle, quiet voice within. Trust what you hear and take action based on this inner guidance. Practice this regularly to strengthen your intuitive connection and embrace the safety found in surrendering to the intuitive, natural flow of your path on your journey through life.

Activity #25

# CANDICE KNIGHT

# LIVING WITH AN AWARENESS OF OUR ARMOR
Embracing Life Authentically

## Chapter 26:
### Honoring Your Growth

---

*"And you know who I want to thank?
I want to thank me – for believing in me
and doing what they said I could not do.
I want to say to myself in front of all these beautiful people,
'Go on, girl, with your bad self. You did that."*

— **Niecy Nash**
2024 Emmy Award Acceptance Speech

As we stand at the threshold of our next adventure, we find ourselves fitted in an armor unlike any we have ever worn before. This finely tailored suit has been forged from the key takeaways and gifts received along our journey. Before stepping into the unknown, let's take a moment for reflection and acknowledgment—a pause to honor the incredible growth we've achieved. The armor, once a weighty burden we endured through a lifetime, has now been lightened. Each lesson, each gift, has contributed to a transformation that deserves recognition. As we embark on the next chapter, may we carry the lightened load with hearts filled, not just with courage, but with the wisdom and self-awareness gained from getting under our armor.

We are taught to be humble and not to brag, but I want you to celebrate your wins—not because you are looking for a first-place ribbon, but because you are absolutely okay with acknowledging how far you

# UNDER THE
# ARMOR

have come. I spent so much time hoping someone else would pat me on the back and comment on the effort I put into whatever I was doing. As a wife, mother, friend, or employee, I tried so hard to be good enough, but no matter what anyone said, there was always a voice of doubt in my mind and a push to be even better at the next opportunity to prove my worth to someone else. Can you see the insanity in this?

I have shared with you the moments in my life that I have been especially proud of, but what holds the greatest significance is how I have been able to move on from the most important relationship I have ever had. Not only was it a transformative union, but it is one that will continue in some way for many years to come because, although we have broken ties, we will forever be connected by our children. I honor my growth because, if not for the commitment I made to face the darkness and remove the weight of my armor, I would not be able to show up the way I do each day for myself and my children.

My ex-husband and I met in early 2001, and I felt that we had a connection that I had never experienced with anyone else. Although there were clear signs that suggested we might have challenges ahead, I wanted to be with him. It is interesting that after the tragedy of September 11, I decided to move back to Toronto to be closer to my family. He and I parted ways, until I found myself back in Windsor to earn a second university degree, and we reconnected in 2003.

It seemed that in no time at all we decided to get married, and we sealed the deal at the very start of 2004, the day after my 29th birthday. After a miscarriage, we welcomed our son into our family in the spring of 2005. It felt that I finally had my happily ever after. Marriage and kids can show you a side of your partner, as well as a side of yourself, that isn't what you expected to see. If you aren't self-aware, then you are bound to pick a partner that will reflect the wounds you have and the reasons why you have armor in the first place. I married my wounds, and he married his. We just didn't know it yet.

Jump ahead almost 16 years and 2 previous separations, the final breakup was almost upon us, but I had no clue it was coming. Or did I? I still have the journal that I was keeping at the time, and right before I was about to leave for that conference in Toronto, I wrote that I wondered if my marriage was over. I had all these hopes and dreams, but I admitted that when I looked to my future, I didn't see him beside me. I wasn't feeling negative; I was simply expressing what was in my heart and allowed the words to flow.

What I have learned from all the lessons I am sharing with you is that there is deep healing when we are able to release our armor from a place of love, and I am so proud of myself for being able to do this. Each layer of armor that I can remove with gratitude and acceptance is more likely to leave me unburdened for the long-term because it is genuine and sincere. From the moment my ex left, I felt that the ending was exactly what needed to happen. It was meant to happen before, but neither of us was quite ready to learn the lesson from one another and move on. I have imagined that we have spent previous lifetimes together, which is why the bond was so strong and so difficult to break.

When I think about this relationship, it feels impossible that we were even together at all. Because of the work I have done to get under layer upon layer of painful armor attached to not only him, but linked to so many other significant men in my life, I can appreciate what we had and wish him well. That is the power of healing.

I moved forward in love. I am so grateful that his soul and mine chose each other to learn from. We have three beautiful children, one who wouldn't even be here if we had learned our lesson sooner. We had a lot of great times together as a couple and as a family, and that is what I choose to hold dear to my heart. But that doesn't dim the truth that

# UNDER THE
# ARMOR

we are better apart than together. His leaving was for him, and I thank him because, in the end, it was for me, as well. I wouldn't be where I am right now or going where I am meant to be if it weren't for him, because of him, and now in the absence of him.

I wish him happiness and health, not only because he is the father of my children, but because he is a person on this planet, and I want to have love for everyone. I have to remind myself of that sometimes when I am shocked by the words, actions, and intentions of people. Many times, I shake my head in dismay, but the more I trust that we are all connected, the more I love myself and allow myself to care, but not be corrupted. I am able to share the energy of love with others without expectation. I believe that it is because of my being able to release the need to get back at my ex or try to make him feel bad about any hurtful things I believe he did, that I am healthy and happy myself.

When someone no longer makes you break down in tears, lash out in rage, or waste time scheming revenge, you know that you have leveled up and removed the toxic remains of the armor associated with them. When you no longer reminisce about the good times or make a mental list of all the bad, you have proof that you have healed in a significant way. When you no longer get triggered and are able to stand strong with no need to say anything at all, you have truly become a warrior. Can you see the difference? **You no longer need a sword to fight since you have learned that there is no longer anything to fight for**. When you get to this point, you should absolutely honor your growth.

You should be proud of yourself. You are no longer in need of someone else to congratulate you. Your heart and soul thank you, and Future You is excited that they'll be able to live out the life they always wanted for you. That couldn't have happened if you hadn't taken the time to shed the tears, face your truth, and get under your armor on your own.

You did this because you finally accepted that no matter who aided you along the way, you chose to accept the help, whether it was delivered through wisdom, guidance, and/or love. Say thank you to yourself right now. To myself I say, "I love you girl, and I am so proud of you!" We got this!

## TRY THIS:
Celebrating Your Growth

Take a moment to reflect on your journey and write down three significant ways you have grown. Acknowledge your accomplishments, no matter how big or small they may seem. Then, look in the mirror and say out loud, "I am proud of you. You've come a long way, and you deserve to celebrate your growth." Make this a regular practice — it will reinforce your self-worth and honor the progress you've made.

Activity #26

# Chapter 27:
## Preparing for the Next Level

*"You only lose what you cling to."*
## — Buddha

Our emotional armor is both protective and confining. Imagine it as a sturdy, layered exterior—a shield formed by past experiences, societal expectations, and personal fears. Each layer represents a coping mechanism or defense developed over time. Like a set of intricately woven chains, each link represents a specific emotional barrier. These chains might be made of experiences, societal norms, or self-imposed limitations. The armor can feel heavy, like carrying the weight of past traumas and expectations on your shoulders.

We've gotten underneath the layers of our armor, but now it's time to carefully dismantle the fine layer of chains. It's an intricate task, requiring ongoing awareness, patience, and self-reflection. It can be tedious at times, but as each link is removed, the emotional weight lessens, revealing even more of the vulnerable, authentic soul beneath.

The process might feel like emerging from a cocoon, allowing the true self to emerge, free from the constraints of the protective but limiting shell. The uncovered soul is resilient, strong, and capable of facing life's challenges with newfound courage. It always has been, and it always will be.

Even though I am proud of releasing what needed to fall away, it hasn't been easy, nor am I finished. Healing is a journey with multiple layers to uncover. No matter how far we believe we have come, there's always another layer waiting to be addressed. Under each layer lies new awareness and wisdom. You are never done removing your armor, and if you're not careful, you might add an extra layer by falling back into old habits.

Not everyone who reads this book will want to delve into the chaos and fight the mental battles as I have. That's okay. This book is for anyone who feels burdened by the weight of their past, has had enough, and believes there is something better on the other side. Your next adventure might not have presented itself yet, but you still need to be prepared because if and when it does, it's because you have proven yourself ready.

I have been preparing for this moment for 30 years. My life path shifted after the fatal car accident at the age of 14. It took a few years to get ready for the next adventure, which brought me to where I currently live. Three decades later, after education, a marriage, career, and guiding two of my three children into their own life adventures, I am ready for mine. This adventure seems more significant than the others.

I have faced life without having a place to go back home to. I proved I could handle the responsibilities of being a student, employee, mother, wife, and citizen. I have braved most days with curiosity, kindness, and appreciation. Most importantly, I no longer shy away from exposing my vulnerable, authentic self because I accept that I am worthy, lovable, and enough to be accepted exactly as I am. I've come a long way, and because I see that, I know I am ready to surrender and say yes to what is next.

To be ready, it might not only be your armor that you need to release.

# UNDER THE
# ARMOR

You don't need to try to find things to dump overboard, although you can begin by going through your belongings and letting go of anything you haven't used in a while or don't love. Decluttering is a great way to clear the way for new and more fitting things to find their way to you. **If you don't release the old, there won't be much room for the new.**

I know I will eventually sell the house I live in. After almost a decade here, there is a lot I don't need to take with me. There are memories to leave behind and items that won't have a place in my next home. Rather than waiting until the last moment, I will be conscious of anything new I bring in and remove whatever I can't imagine taking with me. There are many people who will be happy with what I no longer need.

What else can you shift or remove from your life? What is taking up space or not supporting your growth? Don't worry, you don't have to get rid of everything, but you can move things around, dust them off, and see them from a different perspective. This could be an old antique passed on from your grandmother or a friend you've known since high school. This is where boundaries and priorities can be a good thing to set for yourself.

I used to tell my students, "**Show me your friends, and I'll show you your future.**" Now I'm saying this to you. Are you surrounding yourself with people who are doing what you want to do? If not, make room to meet new people who inspire you. If you don't know what you would like to do now, next time something catches your eye and you feel curious, don't let it go. Ask a friend if you need to, but if no one is available, I hope you go on your own because you have a better chance of meeting someone new.

If you find yourself brought down by the vibe of a friend who spends more time gossiping or judging, get involved in something where you can discuss things that make your heart sing and your mind expand. Go to an art gallery, let yourself be called to a piece of art, and look at it until you hear what it wants you to know. Does this sound crazy? Good! Growth can feel crazy. You are meeting a new side of yourself, and it takes time to become familiar.

To prepare for the next stage, say yes even when you're scared and no even if you feel you should agree. Tune in to yourself and stop questioning what comes up for you. Get curious! Remember, not everything or everyone that started the journey with you or tagged along the way is meant to move forward with you. Brian A.D. Chalker (British country singer, journalist) wrote a poem mentioning that friends come into your life for either a season, a reason, or a lifetime. It's not just friendships though — it can be anything.

We are all here to be of service. I am writing my first book, but that is just an opening to whatever is in store for me next. The more we remove our armor, the better able we are to see our gifts and realize that we benefit when we share them with others. To prepare for the next stage, make sure you can hear the call and are willing to answer it. Acknowledge that you will stumble and fall every now and then. Getting back up, dusting yourself off, and pausing to listen to the whispers of your soul is essential. When in doubt, remind yourself that you're exactly where you are meant to be.

# UNDER THE ARMOR

## TRY THIS:
Leveling Up

Take some time to declutter your space, removing items you no longer use or love, to create room for new opportunities. Reflect on your relationships and consider setting boundaries with those who don't support your growth. Practice saying yes to exciting opportunities, even if they scare you, and no to things that don't serve your higher purpose. Trust your intuition and follow where it leads you.

Activity #27

# Chapter 28:
## Creating the Vision

*"As soon as you trust yourself,
you will know how to live."*

## — Johann Wolfgang von Goethe

The journey of removing the tough outer layers of armor is not just about shedding protection — it's about uncovering the true essence that lies beneath. Each layer we strip away reveals the authentic self, the light that has always been there, waiting to shine brightly. **As you recognize the truth of how much your armor has held you back, you will feel the call of your soul becoming clearer and stronger.** Changes need to be made to live the life you've dreamed of, but never allowed yourself to believe was possible.

You don't need to try to figure it all out at once. Dream and see what comes up for you. When I created my first vision board in 2014, after my breakdown/breakthrough, I had no plan. I started cutting out pictures from magazines that I had intended to recycle, but instead, I found myself creating a vision board. I spent hours cutting out images and words that stood out to me. Once I had cut out all my visuals, I arranged them intuitively. What emerged was a masterpiece that represented my dreams and aspirations.

In 2019, following another marital breakup, I created a second vi-

# UNDER THE ARMOR

sion board. This time, it was different. I felt guided to cut a circle from the bristol board and placed the Celtic triskele symbol in the center, representing the cycles of birth, life, and death. This vision board became a powerful tool during the Covid pandemic when I hosted an online workshop called 'Seeing Beyond 2020.' Participants chose themes for their vision boards and wrote affirmations to amplify their intentions. My word for 2020 was "allow," symbolizing the power of water—healing, cleansing, flowing, and unbreakable.

Instead of using armor, I began to allow myself to meet life's challenges, learning to trust and surrender. Each year since, I have chosen a new power word to guide me. In 2023, those words were "trust" and "surrender." With these words to inspire me, I set intentions that supported my dreams. However, this time, I couldn't create a vision board for my future. I had a collection of new pictures, but no clear vision. My intention was to allow the universe to guide me.

In the past, my armor kept me from dreaming big. **As I got underneath the layers, I allowed myself to imagine a life not solely motivated by security**. The more free I became from my armor, the more I understood what was possible. I used to include butterflies in my vision boards, symbolizing transformation. Now, I am ready to emerge from the cocoon, transformed and prepared for a new life.

I encourage you to see beyond your current armor and set intentions for the life you desire. Connect to the whispers of your intuition and see what your soul has in store for you. Writing your dreams and intentions on paper is a powerful way to set things into motion. Each year, I conduct a New Year's Eve bowl burning ceremony, where I write down what I want to release and set it on fire, symbolizing letting go. I also write a letter to my future self, seal it and read it the following year. This ritual connects me to my creative flow and serves as proof that I have removed enough armor to receive messages from my higher self.

## CANDICE KNIGHT

Our armor doesn't just protect our body and heart — It blocks our connection to our divine source. When you take off the armor, you see beyond perceived limitations and breathe in your desires. Though the brightness of your true self may seem intense at first, you will adjust. You are resilient and ready to meet life with newfound courage.

# UNDER THE ARMOR

## TRY THIS:
### Setting Intentions

Create your own vision board or intention sketchbook. Start by cutting out images, words, and symbols that resonate with you from magazines. Arrange them intuitively on a board or in a sketchbook. Title one page, "Current Me," and draw yourself, adding words and images that represent your present self. On the adjoining page, title it "Future Me" and envision your ideal self, adding positive attributes and goals. This practice will help you visualize and set intentions for your future, making your dreams feel more attainable.

Activity #28

# Chapter 29:
## Fearlessly Moving Forward

*"The treasure you seek is
hidden in the cave you fear to enter."*

— **Joseph Campbell**

There is a parable by American author and motivational speaker, Wayne Dyer, where two fetuses discuss life after birth. One believes in a world beyond the womb, while the other only trusts its current reality. Much like a caterpillar undergoing transformation, change is inevitable. A fetus wouldn't choose birth, nor would a caterpillar choose to dissolve into goo to become a butterfly. Similarly, we hold onto familiar, yet uncomfortable lives. Isn't it time to consider that under that armor is the best of us waiting to emerge?

Have you ever heard the story of the golden Buddha? In 1957, a Thai monastery was being relocated, and as a clay Buddha was being moved some of the clay came off and revealed gold underneath. Historians believe it was covered in clay to protect it from invaders. Hidden under its armor for centuries, it was finally restored to its original splendor.

We are like the golden Buddha. We cover ourselves in armor to protect our most sacred self. If you're reading this, your armor has begun to crack. From those cracks shines a beautiful golden light, signaling it's time to shed the protection that has held you back from joy, abun-

# UNDER THE
# ARMOR

dance, and love.

In 2022, I felt called to get a tattoo of a snake and a butterfly intertwined with the phases of the moon above them and my personal north star below them. Shortly afterward, I added the constellation of my astrological sign to complete the picture. This is what this tattoo means to me —

The snake is symbolic of releasing what we have outgrown. If a snake does not shed its skin, it can no longer live. Life is a process of growth and release. The cycles of the moon represent this cycle. The snake is also a symbol of continuous renewal of life and fertility, yet its venom is both a poison and an antidote. We are like that as well when we become our own worst enemy and then our greatest healer.

My north star is what guides me and, although my ancestors did not follow this star to find their freedom, it is the guide to my own personal freedom. If I don't know which way to go, I only need to look within for the guidance of my soul. The butterfly is a symbol that, not only was I reborn to start a new phase of my life, but that was just one aspect of the many phases of my personal transformation. What is coming now requires me to use the wings I have developed over the last decade and use them to fly.

You've survived so much. Obstacles won't disappear, but you'll find you don't need the armor anymore because you've tapped into the strength of your soul. As you allow it to shine, you'll discover you're never alone.

Throughout this book, I have been real, genuine and authentic, with you. I have been raw in my honest vulnerability, and I hope that you have been able to relate to me and my experiences in some way. I am no more resilient than you. My armor weighed me down for far too long and, although I might wish that some parts of my life hadn't left such a deep wound to heal, I wouldn't change anything. My life has brought me here and your life has brought you to this point alongside me. There is no going back. My family can't return from the dead, the pain people brought to my life cannot be erased, and my mistakes cannot be taken back.

You are ready to move beyond the cover of armor. You will stumble, but you'll never revert to your old self. You'll catch yourself complaining, then notice the beauty around you. When you see someone diminishing themselves, you'll reassure them, because you've been there.

When you worry about the future, you'll take a deep breath and return to the present moment. You've got this. Look in the mirror and notice the sparkle in your eyes – it's your soul, alive and shining.

We're not done with our healing journey as long as we live. Each lesson learned brings a new one. We might still become afraid at times, but our self-awareness and love for ourselves enable us to face the unknown with courage, without relying on emotional armor for protection.

Turn to the future. You are and always will be a warrior. Let your inner child know that they are safe. Shine brightly because the world needs you. Thank you for being you.

# UNDER THE
# ARMOR

## TRY THIS:
## Fearlessly Moving Forward

Visualize the next stage of your life as a journey through an unexplored forest. As you walk, imagine facing obstacles — fallen branches, muddy paths, and streams to cross. Instead of turning back, find ways to navigate each challenge, trusting your intuition to guide you. When you encounter a roadblock, pause, strategize, and look beyond the immediate problem for a solution. Reflect on each obstacle you overcome, recognizing the growth and resilience you gain with every step forward. This practice helps you build confidence in your ability to face the unknown and reinforces your commitment to move forward without the weight of your old armor.

Activity #29

# Chapter 30:
## Embracing Your Authentic Journey

*"Healing is an art.
It takes time, it takes practice.
It takes love."*

**— Maza Dohta**

As we come to the end of this part of the journey, it's important to pause and reflect on what we've explored together. We've examined the emotional armor we wear, the layers we've built to protect ourselves from pain, and the courage it takes to begin shedding those defenses. Each chapter of this book has taken us deeper into understanding not just the purpose of our armor but also the power of vulnerability and the freedom that comes with breaking free from those layers.

One key takeaway from this exploration is that our emotional armor, while seemingly protective, often prevents us from living fully. It blocks us from forming deeper connections with others, from expressing our true selves, and from experiencing the richness of life. Our armor gives us a sense of control, but it also keeps us trapped in fear—fear of rejection, fear of failure, and, ultimately, fear of being seen for who we really are. But as we've discovered, it's through embracing our vulnerabilities that we find our true strength.

In reflecting on my personal journey, I have come to understand that

# UNDER THE
# ARMOR

healing is not linear. The process of dismantling armor is ongoing. At times, the layers fall away quickly, while at other times, they cling to us, refusing to budge without intense effort. But the cracks in our armor are where the light gets in, where healing begins. It's where we start to reclaim the parts of ourselves we've hidden away for too long.

To everyone who has read this book, I hope you now see that you are not alone in this process. We all wear armor, and we all have our own stories of struggle and resilience. Whether your armor was forged by childhood wounds, traumatic experiences, or the relentless pressures of adulthood, know that you have the power to begin shedding those layers. You are capable of facing your fears and embracing a life filled with authenticity, love, and connection.

As we conclude, I want to leave you with a message of hope and encouragement. The journey to break free from your armor is not easy, but it is worth it. It takes courage to confront the parts of yourself that have been hidden away for so long, but in doing so, you reclaim your power. You allow yourself to be seen, heard, and loved—not just by others, but by yourself. You step into a life that is fuller, richer, and more aligned with who you truly are.

Throughout this journey, remember to be patient and gentle with yourself. Healing is a process that requires time and grace. There will be setbacks, moments of doubt, and times when you want to retreat behind your armor. But each step forward, no matter how small, is a victory. Each moment of vulnerability brings you closer to the freedom you seek.

Thank you for allowing me to walk alongside you in this journey. My hope is that the stories and strategies shared in this book have inspired you to continue your path of self-discovery. Remember, the greatest comeback of your life is not only possible, but it is waiting for you on the other side of your armor. The time has come to shed those layers and step into the life you were always meant to live.

Here are some practical steps to apply what you've learned:

**DAILY REFLECTION** — Spend a few minutes each day reflecting on your emotions and experiences. Journaling can be a powerful tool to track your progress and maintain self-awareness.

**SET CLEAR INTENTIONS** — Regularly revisit and update your vision board or intention journal. Allow yourself to dream big and visualize the life you desire.

**EMBRACE VULNERABILITY** — Practice being open and honest in your relationships. Share your true self with those you trust, and allow yourself to receive love and support.

**SEEK SUPPORT** — Don't hesitate to seek help when needed. Whether through therapy, support groups, or trusted friends, sharing your journey with others can provide additional strength and perspective.

Your courage, resilience, and willingness to embrace your true self are the greatest gifts you can offer to the world.

Shine brightly, warrior. The world needs your light.

Love,
**Candice**

For more information please visit
www.candiceknight.ca

# Afterward

*"Let the mystery remain a mystery."*
— **Richard Wagamese**

*January 2025*

Earlier this month, I celebrated my 50th birthday, and one thing stood out: how much I cried. I cried each time I spoke with a friend or family member and through my smiles as I read the birthday greetings on my social media page. I wasn't crying because I felt old. So, why was I crying?

I missed what I had left behind—my older children, my home, my friends, the walking trails, and the businesses where I had built meaningful relationships. Part of me missed my past, and I think another part didn't want to let go, as though holding on would make the transition to this new life easier.

In October, I moved to British Columbia from Ontario. This manuscript was written back in April, and so much has unfolded since then. I want to share what happened after I took that leap of faith I'd been building up to for years.

At first, I landed gently, with joy and hope in my heart. But eventually, grief set in, and the dream I had envisioned began to feel less like a dream come true and more like a "What have I done?" moment.

# UNDER THE ARMOR

All my deepest fears surfaced, haunting me with doubt. Yet, despite the fear, I had no regrets. Deep down, I knew I was meant to make this change, and I held on to the hope that, one day, it would all make sense—or at least I hoped it would. The fear was strong, though, and there were many nights when I tossed and turned, worrying about my children and myself.

I reminded myself that, no matter what, I could always return to teaching. Still, that thought felt like admitting defeat. I'll be honest: I did apply for my teaching certificate, but I promised myself I'd only do occasional or substitute teaching when needed. After all, a little income wouldn't hurt as I worked to create my own flow of finances.

Almost daily, I questioned what I wanted to do with my life. I thought I knew, but part of me doubted whether I had the drive to stick with it long enough to turn my vision into something profitable. My biggest fear was that no one would want what I had to offer and that I'd never make enough to support myself. That thought—the one questioning my ability to succeed—was what most often drove me to question my sanity. For the first time in my adult life, I didn't have a steady job providing consistent income. I had to be responsible for myself in ways I wasn't sure I could manage, and I truly believed I would struggle.

Another wound revealed itself during this transition: my need to please others. Since arriving in Kelowna, I've met some amazing people, but I've also encountered a few triggers tied to my past trauma. Thankfully, I've been able to reflect on my feelings, recognizing the younger version of me who was desperate for validation and would dismiss her own needs to avoid upsetting others.

How is all of this possible? I have more healing to do. I already knew that, but I didn't expect the lessons to be so obvious—or so blunt.

Recording the audiobook has been an incredible experience. I can confidently say the advice in this book is solid. In fact, I needed to read my own words! As I said earlier, not everything will apply to your life, but I'm confident there are lessons I've learned that will benefit you, too. After all, we're not so different.

In recent days, something has shifted within me, and I'm grateful for the chance to write this final note before the book goes to the publisher next month. I've decided to fill myself with positive energy. I imagine it as a golden, sparkly warmth radiating from my core, spreading through my body, and into the world around me. When I visualize this, I tell myself I'm "getting my gold up." Silly as it may sound, it's helping.

I've become extra mindful of my thoughts and emotions, making a conscious effort to catch myself when I fall into a spiral of negativity. I truly believe we attract what we focus on most. Negative thinking, fear, anger, and doubt won't lead to a higher state of being. In 2025, my daily practice will be to visualize my highest and best self—confident, joyful, loving, and at peace.

I don't have all the answers, but I'm committed to saying yes to the experiences and people who feel like they're meant to guide me forward. I'm also going to slow down and allow myself to feel so that I can heal. I can't push through any longer.

I've also written a prayer that I recite daily to align my mind and heart. As I fill myself with that golden glow, I imagine it lighting up the path ahead, making it clearer and more vibrant. I can't wait to see what unfolds!

# UNDER THE ARMOR

If you'd like to join me on this journey—if you're looking for support as you create or embrace change in your own life—I invite you to reach out. Let's connect. I'm sending you so much love.

Thank you for reading this book, for sharing it with others, and most of all, for investing time in your own personal growth. I wish you all the best.

With love,
**Candice**

# Resources

## Books

- Spirit Talker by Shawn Leonard
- Your Soul's Plan by Robert Schwartz
- The Celestine Prophecy Series by James Redfield
- The Surrender Experiment by Michael A Singer
- Black Girl in Love with Herself by Trey Anthony
- The Secret by Rhonda Byrne
- Wise Power by Alexandra Pope & Sjanie Hugo Wurlitzer
- Change Your Thoughts, Change Your Life by Dr. Wayne Dyer
- Dying to be Me by Anita Moorjani
- God on a Harley by Joan Brady
- The Body Mind Workbook by Debbie Shapiro
- The Soul of Money by Lynne Twist
- You Were Not Born to Suffer by Blake D Bauer
- Embers by Richard Wagamese
- Spirit Guides and Angel Guardians by Richard Webster

## Oracle Decks

- The Light Seers Tarot by Chris - Anne
- The Power of Surrender Cards by Judith Orloff, M.D.
- The Sacred Creators Oracle by Chris - Anne
- Sacred Destiny by Denise Linn
- Secrets of the Ancestors by Abiola Abrams
- Wisdom of the Oracle by Collette Baron-Reid
- The Hero's Journey Dream Oracle by Kelly Sullivan Walden
- Sacred Rebels Oracle by Alana Fairchild